FULDA

Guide

BY ANTON SCHMITT
AND THOMAS SCHMITT

TRANSLATED BY
EBERHARD PAUL

VERLAG PARZELLER · FULDA

ISBN 3 7900 0273 9

Photos by Erich Gutberlet, Großenlüder;
and Rolf Kreuder, Tann, page 18; Hans Retzlaff,
Tann, p. 39; Hubert Weber, Fulda, p. 61
Manufactured by: Druckerei Parzeller, Fulda

TABLE OF CONTENTS

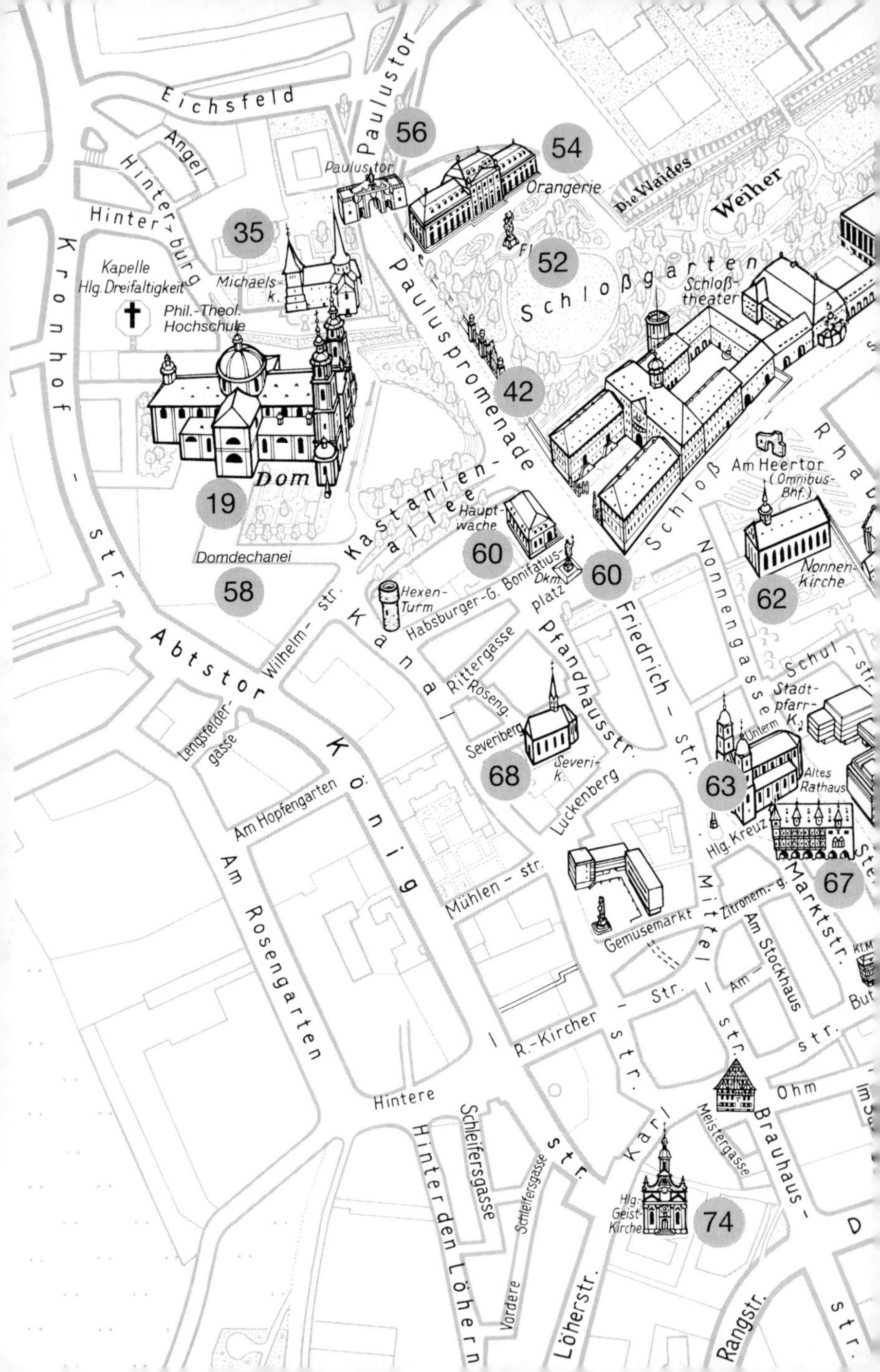

Eichsfeld
Paulustor
56
54
Angel
Hinterburg
Paulustor
Orangerie
Die Waides
Weiher
35
Kapelle
Hlg. Dreifaltigkeit
Michaels-k.
52
Schloßgarten
Schloß-theater
Kronhof-str.
Phil.-Theol. Hochschule
Paulus-promenade
42
Dom
19
Kastanien-allee
Haupt-wache
Am Heertor (Omnibus-Bhf.)
Schloß
Rhab
60
60
Bonifatius-Dkm.
Nonnen-Kirche
62
Domdechanei
58
Hexen-Turm
Habsburger-G.
platz
Friedrich-str.
Nonnengasse
Wilhelm-str.
Kanal
Abtstor
Rittergasse
Roseng.
Pfandhausstr.
Schul-str.
Stadt-pfarr-K.
Unterm
Lengsfelder-gasse
Severiberg
Severi-K.
68
63
Altes Rathaus
Königstr.
Luckenberg
Am Hopfengarten
Hlg. Kreuz
Mühlen-str.
67
Am Rosengarten
Gemüsemarkt
Zitronem.-g.
Marktstr.
Mittel-str.
Am Stockhaus
R.-Kircher-Str.
Am
str.
Ohm
Hintere
Schleifersgasse
Karl-str.
Meistergasse
Brauhaus-
Schleifersgasse
Hlg. Geist-Kirche
74
Hinter den Löhern
Vordere
Löherstr.
Rangstr.
str.

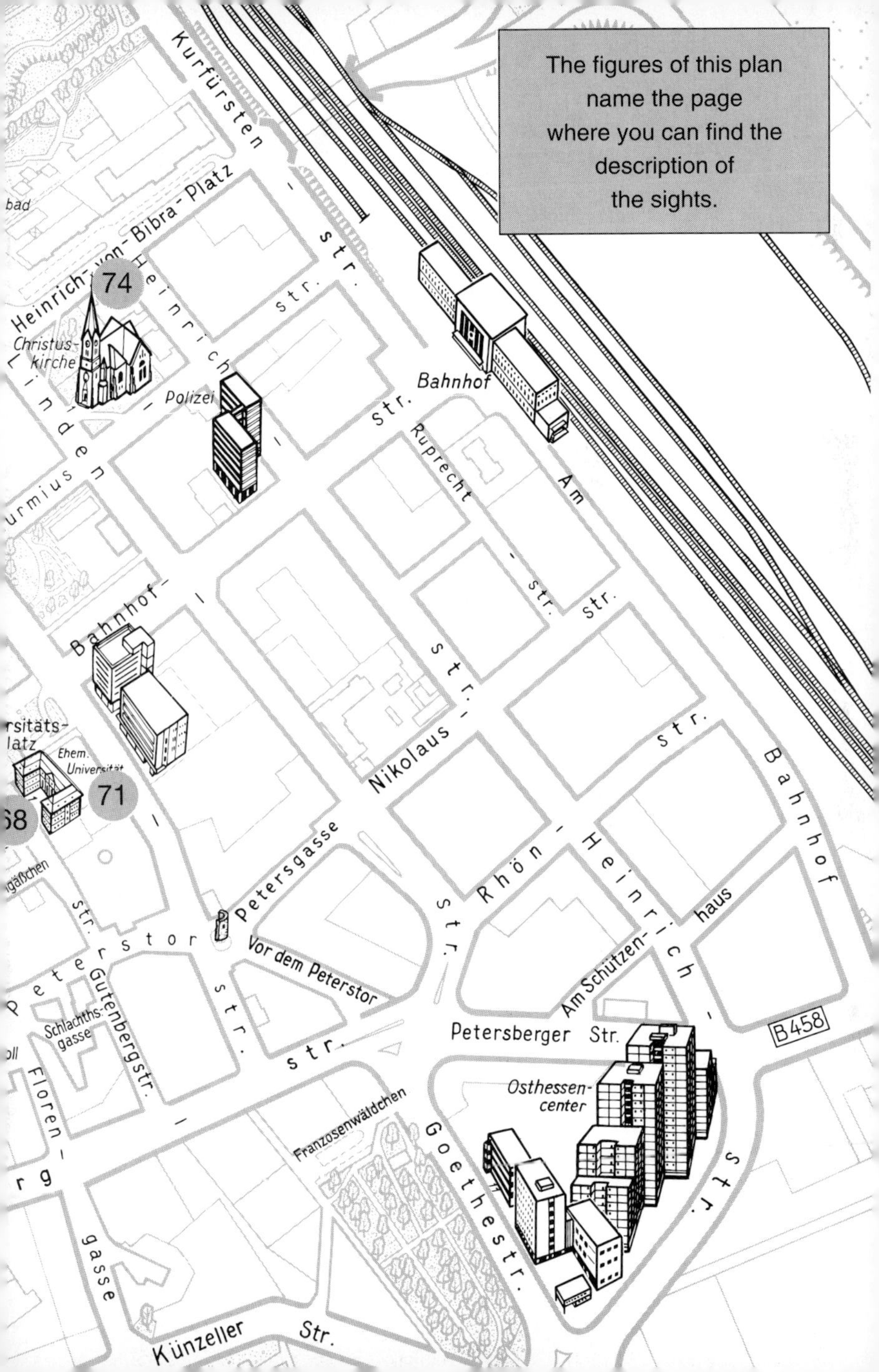

The figures of this plan name the page where you can find the description of the sights.
Kurfürsten - str.
Heinrich - von - Bibra - Platz
Heinrich - str.
74
Christus-kirche
Linden
Polizei
Bahnhof
str.
Ruprecht - str.
Am
str.
Bahnhof -
Ehem. Universität
71
Nikolaus str.
Petersgasse
Rhön - Heinrich -
Bahnhof
haus
Am Schützen-
str.
Peterstor
Vor dem Peterstor
Gutenbergstr.
Schlachths-gasse
str.
Petersberger Str.
B458
Osthessen-center
Franzosenwäldchen
Goethestr.
str.
gasse
Künzeller Str.

FULDA

Venerable and famous for its cultural traditions, looks back at more than 1250 years. At the very beginnings of Germany's history it was its eminent centre.
The Fulda Benedictine convent saw its first and most fruitful flowering immediately after its foundation (744), soon becoming one of the most important focal points where ancient Roman and Christian European cultural traditions merged.
Today Fulda's townscape nevertheless is shaped by another, much later period: Fulda is

THE CITY OF BAROQUE

Its Cathedral, radiating Roman-Baroque feeling, the Orangery in its purest and maturest shape with the wide flight of stairs and the charming Flora in front of it, a jewel of German Baroque sculpturing, offer unforgettable impressions.
The unbroken creative power of that period has brought forth the town's unique, extraordinarily harmonical Baroque quarters.

THE CITY OF ST. BONIFACE

His monument opposite the Palace points to his significance for Fulda. Winfrith – his original name – was born at Crediton/Wessex at about 673. He was educated by Benedictine monks first at Essex Monastery, later at Nursling, where he was ordained a priest. After a futile attempt to convert the Frisians he travelled to Rome where Pope Gregory II gave him his new name, Boniface, and he was entrusted with missionary work among the Franks (719). Three years

Flora Vase in front of the Orangery

later he was consecrated a bishop. The same pope made him an archbishop (732) and a pontifical legate (738). Boniface set himself the task to organize the young Frankian Church and to establish firm ties with Rome. For this reason he founded a great number of dioceses and, in 744, he had the Fulda convent founded: After becoming Bishop of Mainz (Mayance) he started for a last missionary enterprise to Frisia, where he was murdered in 754. His body was brought to Fulda where he found his grave in its convent church.

FULDA CHRONICLE

744	March 12th, Fulda's convent founded by Sturmius
751	exemption from episcopal rule granted by Pope Zachary
754	Boniface martyred in Frisia
774	immunity from secular rule granted to the convent
779	Sturmius dies
791–819	building of Abbot Ratgar's basilica, then the largest north of the Alps
820 – 822	rotunda of St. Michael's erected
822 – 842	Rabanus Maurus is Fulda's fifth abbot
969	Fulda's abbots are awarded the title of Primate of Benedictine Convents throughout Germany and Gaul
1019	Fulda granted market, toll and coinage rights by Emperor Heinrich II
1020	Emperor Heinrich II and Pope Benedict VIII visit Fulda together
1157	Fulda granted a town charter by Emperor Friedrich Barbarossa; a diet is held in Fulda by the Emperor
1220	Emperor Friedrich II elevates the abbots to the rank of imperial princes

St. Boniface monument

SCT. BONIFACIUS
GERMANORUM APOSTOLUS

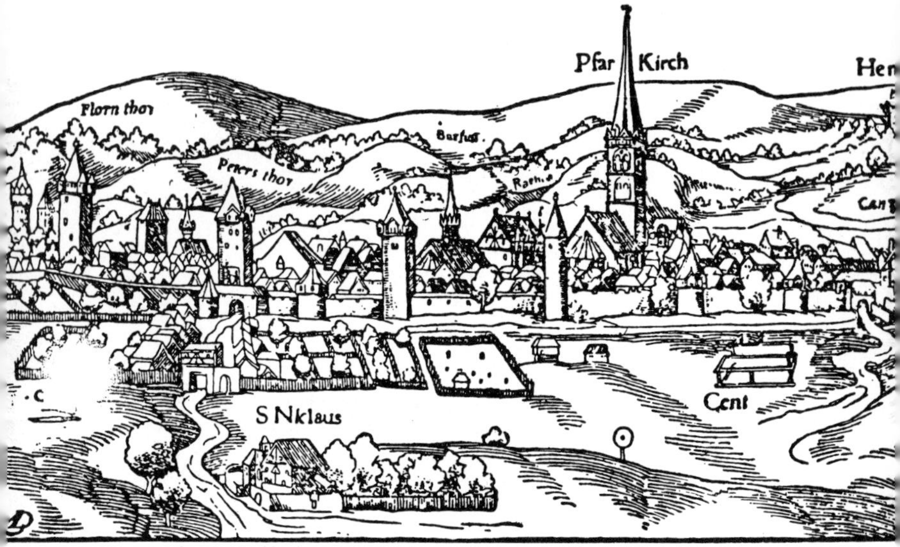

The city of Fulda about 1500 (Brosamer)

1237	first Franciscan friary in Fulda
about 1300	Abbot Heinrich von Weilnau builds a castle on the site of today's city palace
1331	a revolt of Fulda's citizens against the abbot fails
1350	the Black Death in Fulda
1356	the title of Arch Chancellors to the Empress awarded to the abbots by Emperor Karl IV
1525	Peasants'Revolt; monasteries in and around Fulda devastated
1571	Jesuits called to Fulda
1584	Pontifical Seminary of the Jesuits established to support the Counter-Reformation
1620	Franciscans return to Fulda
1626	Benedictine nuns arrive; they move to their new church and convent buildings in 1631
1631	Gustav Adolf of Sweden gives the Fulda principality to the Landgrave of Hesse who carries off and destroys the famous old convent library

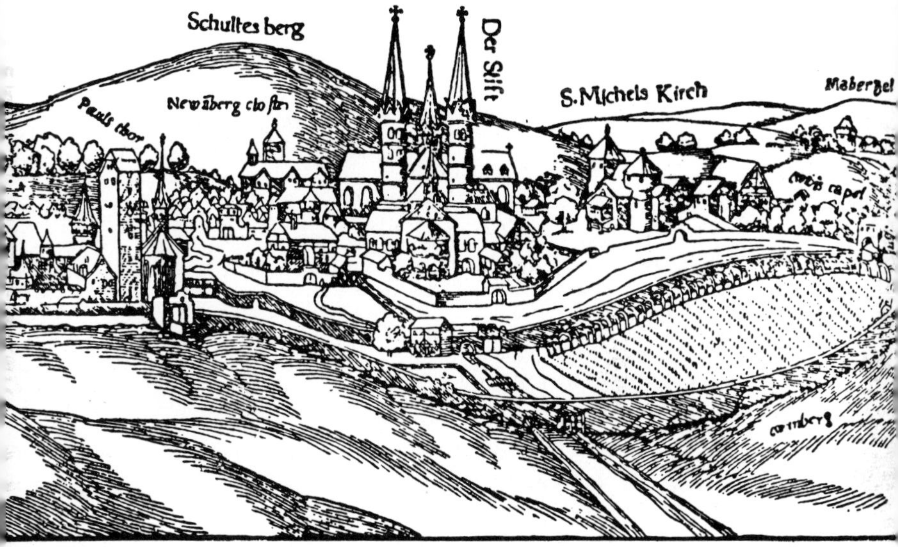

1634	the principality is returned to the prince abbot
1668	new buildings erected for the Benedictine convent (today the home of the Episcopal Seminary
1704–1712	Johann Dientzenhofer erects today's Cathedral on the foundation walls of Ratgar's old collegiate church
1706–1714	the city palace erected
1722	the Orangery building begun
1723	Compulsory school attendance for boys introduced
1734	University founded
1741	fayence manufacture established
1752	Diocese of Fulda founded; the abbots become prince bishops
1758	Main Guard House built
1758–1762	church and convent buildings on Frauenberg erected
1764	porcelain manufacture takes the place of the for-

	mer fayence production; it is dissolved again in 1789
1770–1786	Fulda's main parish church (Stadtpfarrkirche) built
1803	In consequence of the secularization of ecclesiastical principalities Fulda loses its independence; the new ruler is Prince Wilhelm V of Orange-Nassau
1810–1813	Fulda becomes a department of the Grand Duchy of Frankfurt under Karl von Dalberg
1815	After the Vienna Congress the territory of Fulda's old principality is divided among Bavaria, Hesse-Darmstadt, the Hessian Electorate and Saxe-Meiningen-Eisenach
1866	Fulda together with the Hesse Electorate annexed by Prussia; the first railway line reaches Fulda in that year
1867	The Fulda Bishops' Conference convenes for the first time
1875–1884	in consequence of the struggle between the Catholic Church and the Prussian state the Franciscans are expelled from Fulda
1938	the Synagogue burnt down by the Nazis
1940	Franciscans expelled again; they return in 1945
1944 and 1945	allied air raids on Fulda
1945	Fulda occupied by American troops
1946	first expellees from the eastern German provinces arrive
1949	Protestant German Church Congress establishes its permanent offices in Fulda
1954	76th German Catholic Congress in Fulda
1972	24 neighbouring communities incorporated; the number of inhabitants reaches almost 60.000
1980	Pope John Paul II visits Fulda

Frauenberg convent from the Fulda meadows

FULDA TODAY

When Fulda was occupied by the U.S. Army on April 1, 1945, it had suffered heavily by the war. 1208 men had lost their lives fighting, 1586 of its inhabitants had been killed in air raids and about 900 more were missing. Almost one third of its living quarters had been destroyed. Nevertheless, the number of inhabitants had not decreased, as more than 5.000 evacuees from other parts of Germany had found shelter within its walls. In 1946 3.000 expellees from Germany's eastern provinces arrived. With the re-union of families and a steady influx of evacuees from the surrounding countryside who found work in Fulda's industry their total number in Fulda rose to 10.000. In 1939, 32.000 people had lived in the town, after the war there were 45.000. By the incorporation of 24 communities on August 1, 1972, the number of inhabitants rose to 60.000.
Petersberg and Künzell, two communities that are economically parts of the town but have not been incorporated, are growing rapidly. Together with these communities that form a coherent urban area with Fulda the number of inhabitants today is about 90.000. The fact that any larger city is more than 100 km away underlines an economic importance as the centre of eastern Hesse that by far exceeds its size.
Fulda is of great importance as a religious centre for both Christian denominations in Germany. The German Catholic bishops have their regular annual conferences in Fulda and it is also the seat of the Presidential Office of the German Protestant Church Congress. At the same time it is the seat of a Roman Catholic bishop and as such the centre for one of the three Hessian dioceses.
The Catholic Church maintains 20 parishes within the city boundaries. Among the houses of religious orders the most important are the Franciscan convent on Frauenberg as the seat of the Thuringian Province of that order, the boarding school of the Marian Brothers, the Benedictine Abbey of St. Mary, the mother house of the Sisters of Mercy of St. Vincent de Paul, and the school of the Mary Ward Sisters.

Fulda is also the seat of the Protestant dean for Fulda and Hünfeld. There are 7 Protestant parishes in the town.
Fulda has always been a city of schools. The traditions of the former convent schools and the Pontifical Seminary have been continued by the Pontifical Theological Faculty and the Episcopal Seminary. Fulda College – as such established in 1974 – teaches applied informatics and mathematics, electrical engineering, home economics, food technology, social sciences, and economics.
Fulda's museums are the Municipal Vonderau Museum (Museum Building at Jesuitenplatz) a regional museum with considerable prehistoric exhibits and with treasures from Fulda's political and art history as well as the Anton Schmitt Collection of Graphical Arts; more museums are the German Fire Brigade Museum and the Cathedral Museum. The Historical Rooms in the City Palace together with its Kaisersaal, Fürstensaal and the Cabinet of Mirrors are also particularly worth seeing. The Landesbibliothek (Hessian State Library) takes great pride in its collection of manuscripts from the early and late Middle Ages. There is also one of the rare early Gutenberg Bibles.
Outside the city walls, near the suburb of Bronzell, is the former summer residence, Fasanery Palace. Besides its considerable collection of antiques it renders an excellent idea of princely representation and life style in the first half of the 19th century.
Fulda is also an administrative and a medical centre for a large hinterland. As a regular stop for ICE and IC trains and with its direct access to the Fulda-Würzburg motorway („Rhönlinie") it enjoys excellent traffic connections and, due to its central location within Germany, it is a favourite venue for congresses.
Fulda is the seat of an independent chamber of commerce and it forms the economic centre of eastern Hesse for about 320.000 people. Fulda enjoys a manifold , mainly middle-class economic structure and healthy sociological conditions. Textile industry holds the first place. It had its origins in the once considerable home industry of linen weavers in the Fulda area at the beginning of the 19th century, when more than 10.000 looms were at work. Today its main products are carpeting, heavy textiles, industrial felts and technical textiles. Another important industrial branch is the manufacture of special machinery and various metal articles.

A large factory produces rubber tyres. „Fulda-Tyres" are known all over the world.
One important factory for the production of candles and similar wax products is the only remains of a branch that once employed a great number of workers.
Other works produce paints and varnishings, electric motors, woodwind instruments and building materials and there is also a number of printing works. After the war measuring and control technology and machine and tool making factories were founded. Recently enterprises producing paper and packing material and food industry have been added.
Trade and workshops are represented by a great variety of occupations and give evidence of Fulda as the economic centre of a large region. Wholesalers, department stores and the central administration of a chain of retailers underline this. The same is true for Fulda as a banking place: The Hessian Central Bank maintains one of its main branches, the national banks are represented by their own branches, moreover communal savings banks and cooperative financial institutions have their seats in the town.
The fact that Fulda has not only been able to overcome its war damages, but has taken a much more favourable development than former times could have foreseen, owes much to the industry and responsible civic commitment of its citizens, but also to an exemplary municipal administration that has shaped the urban development by developing new residential areas and concentrating economy and industry in the region to make Fulda the metropolis of eastern Hesse. But also the City has undergone a considerable renewal . Pedestrian districts have been established and recently extended. The building boom in the 1950s and 1960s has left a number of incongruous buildings within the town centre that do not fit in the traditional townscape. Nevertheless, the ancient private and public buildings are preserved with loving care both by the citizens themselves and the municipal administration. It is not least due to this that Fulda is so endearing and makes a visit an unforgettable experience.

Heertor: Germany's oldest city gate with Nonnenkirche

FULDA'S SIGHTS

THE CATHEDRAL
(St. Salvator)

The burial church of St. Boniface, the episcopal cathedral, deserves the first rank among Fulda's sights, due both to its importance for art history and its spiritual significance.

Building History

On Sept. 4th, 1700, the Fulda Prince Abbot Adalbert von Schleiffras concluded a contract with the Bamberg architect Johann Dientzenhofer appointing him the prince's court architect. Dientzenhofer had just returned from a journey to Rome that was not without consequences for his architectural conceptions for the design of the Cathedral. The ancient Carolingian collegiate church was pulled down at the same time with the exception of that part of the masonry that became integrated into the new building . It had been in a poor state, but not at all delapidated in the full sense of the word. Schleiffras himself had great influence on the planning. The building contract was concluded in 1704. In 1707 the masonry had been finished and on August 14th, 1712 the edifice was consecrated by its builder. It has been called a cathedral only after the elevation of the Fulda abbots to the rank of prince bishops in 1752.

The Outer Aspect

A brief look at the Cathedral from Paulusallee or Michaelsberg conveys a clear impression of the fundamental shape of the building without, however, revealing the perfection of the interior design. We see the basilical layout of the nave which considerably exceeds in height the aisles with their slanting roofs abutting on it. It receives its light through the windows above the aisles. The transept intersects the aisles to the full height of the nave. The crossing is crowned by the dome which squats rather deeply in the roofs, but with

Pestsäule

its sides free between the diagonal lines of the roofs, where it has huge windows. The arrangement of the aisle windows and their structuring by pilasters indicates the rhythm of its interior articulation. It is the side view that impresses the viewer by the extraordinary tranquillity and noble serenity of the building and the harmony of its proportions. Likewise, the interrelation between the dimensions of the towers, cupolas and turrets are characteristic for a balanced design.
Let us have a closer look at the front (eastern facade). We notice the short distance between the two towers, which is much greater in other Baroque churches. We already know that it is due to maintaining the old towers. But how ingeniously has the architect made a virtue of necessity! By annexing the two side-chapels he gave the required width to the building and by erecting the two obelisks he arranged the whole facade within an imaginary equilateral triangle whose sides pass from the apex of the pediment over the cupolas of the side chapels to the tops of the obelisks.
The addition of the two side chapels to the eastern facade gives the building a very pleasing and at the same time unusual aspect. Clearly and calmly structured by horizontal ledges it nevertheless is dominated by vertical lines.
The pillars of the projection are continued by flower vases on the pediment, making the whole edifice seem lighter with increasing height; in the lower storey heavy Doric columns, but higher up elaborate capitals. The towers, square in their lower parts, pass into a lighter octagonal shape crowned by elegant tower helmets relieved by two lanterns.
The ground floor of the towers is adorned by the huge sandstone statues of St. Boniface and St. Sturmius. flanking the large central window are the patron saints of Fulda, the holy knights Simplicius and Faustinus. At the apex of the pediment the giant figure of the Saviour occupies a dominant position. (Like the first and second collegiate churches, the Cathedral is dedicated to the Saviour.) Above the main portal two angels flanking the coat of arms of the builder, Adalbert von Schleiffras. Creator of the sculptures on the outside is Andreas Balthasar Weber, while the coat of arms group was executed by Balthasar Esterbauer, sculptor from Würzburg, at the beginning of the 18th century.

The Layout

The layout is a combination of a centralized building and the nave, and has been essentially conditioned by the inclusion of parts of the preceding basilica. The old towers have been given a Baroque appearance. The transepts are much shorter than usual, Instead, the side annexes of the Lady Chapel and the vestry extend farther, standing on the foundation walls of the old western transept of the Carolingian basilica. The straight execution of the aisles beyond the crossing are another consequence of depending on the ground plan of the old building. Also the orientation of the church towards the west (instead of the east, as usual) can only be understood by the layout of the old basilica. There, the main altar dedicated to the Saviour was in the east choir. After finishing the basilica the relics of St. Boniface were transferred to the west choir, thus becoming the real centre of the building, determining everything else from then on.

The Interior

Roman influence on the interior can be recognized by the emphasis on the cupola and the space arrangement of the nave. It is structured by alternating short and wide bays; the strictly separated aisles have access from the nave by alternating round arches and narrow passages. In the recesses above the latter are statues of the apostles. The space under the cupola integrates nave and transept. The chancel and the former monks choir behind it repeat the structuring in bays.

The sculptures in the interior and of most altars are mainly by Artari (statues of the apostles, figures in the St. Andrew's and St. John's Chapels, the angels in the cupolas and the attendant figures) and Johannes Neudecker the Elder (St. Boniface Altar in the crypt, Assumption of Mary above the High Altar, David and Isaiah next to the High Altar and the statues of St. Benedict and St. Sturmius at their respective altars). The frescoes of the Evangelists in the spandrels of the cupola are by Columba as well as the medaillons depicting the Prophets in the transept. The rest of the murals in the chapel cupolas in both aisles are by Melchior Steidl.

The nave lacks all the charming architectonic details of the aisles and, due to the arrangement of the High Altar in front of the monks choir, it is also much shorter. The barrel vault of the ceiling has no orna-

The main portal

ments except the plain stucco reglets. The space is beautifully enlivened by the architect's dividing the nave into alternating long and short arches with corresponding small rectangular passages and wide archways on the sides. Everything in the nave aims at concentrating one's attention on the space below the cupola in the crossing and the High Altar behind it.

In the lobby-shaped room below the organ loft two niches contain statues of the popes Gregory II and Zachary by Artari in remembrance of their special relations to St. Boniface. On a column at the eastern end of the nave a Gothic relief of Charlemagne from the old basilica. The staircase in the opposite corner leads into the eastern crypt of the old convent church (no admittance).
On the organ loft a beautifully carved organ screen (1712–1713).The organ has recently been restored to its original Baroque sound (1995/96).
Advancing in the nave towards the High Altar we regard on both sides between the pilaster pairs of the short arches the apostle statues of classical beauty. On the left, Simon, Bartholomew, James the Younger, on the right Thaddeus, Thomas and Philippus, all by Artari with the exception of St. Thomas, the work of the same unknown artist who also created the images of Joseph and Joaquim in the baptistery .The stucco figures above the arcade arches leading to the aisles are symbolic representations of the Fruits of the Holy Ghost. In the pillar next to the pulpit a Late Gothic relief of „Our Lady with the Protective Coat". The pulpit is a masterpiece of Baroque carving with a particularly elaborate soundboard. The wonderful wood carvings of the pulpit as well as those of the organ screen are by Andreas Balthasar Weber, the cabinet work by Georg Blank.
We step under the cupola. In the centre of the floor a medieval round sandstone slab with four hands pointing in the directions of the compass, the so-called Oath-Slab. On this spot the vassals of Fulda are said to have sworn the oath of allegiance to their prince abbots.
More than 55 meters (180 feet) above our heads the symbol of the Holy Ghost is supended in the lantern of the cupola in the shape of a dove. In the niches over the arches of the crossing angel statues by Artari representing the three archangels and the guardian angel. Of particular splendour are the panels in the cupola spandrels with their wonderfully fresh frescoes. In audaciously lively attitudes and realistic imagery they depict the four Evangelists floating on clouds in apocalyptic enrapture. The wall paintings are by Columba, who also executed the medaillons of the Prophets in the aisles and the chancel.

The main altar

Next to the central pillars tombs of Fulda's prince abbots. In the south-east corner that of Placidus von Droste. To the right of the High Altar the Dalberg monument, erected in 1732. The alabaster sculptures have been executed in Neudecker's workshop by Christian Joseph Winterstein from Hadamar. The monument depicting the prince kneeling before the crucifix was put up in his own lifetime.
To the left of the High Altar is the monument to the builder of the Cathedral, Adalbert von Schleiffras, erected in 1722 in blue-black marble with alabaster figures. It is the most beautiful of all tombs in the church and must be regarded as a work of the highest rank. It is a masterpiece by Joh. Heinr. Ernst Mockstatt, sculptor and etcher in Fulda. The figures are executed in marvellous detail and seem to be in winged movement. At the sides are the allegories of Faith and Hope, while Love is lifting up the copper relief of the deceased to hang it on the wall. The figure of Death lies prostrated on the ground.
The High Altar. The chancel is separated from the transept and the aisles by marble balustrades. On both sides on high marble pedestals the alabaster figures of the Prophets David and Isaiah by Neudecker. In the niches of the panels separating the altar from the choir behind it, the figures of the Apostles Peter and Paul by Artari. Over the arches of the gallery, the images of Moses and Isaiah. The black marble pillars of the High Altar, all in one piece, bear the entablature on which the wood-carved group representing Mary's Assumption to Heaven rises. Prominent volutes dissolve into clouds carrying Mary up to Heaven. The clouds are enlivened by putti and flanked by two cherubs. The master of this carving is Neudecker. Its counterpart on the ceiling is a stucco group by Artari, the Holy Trinity awaiting the Virgin Mary to be crowned in Heaven.
Behind the High Altar is the former monk's choir. The finely carved retable holds a copy of the Lord's Supper by Rubens in the Brera palace in Milan. The magnificent walnut choir stalls of severe design have nothing of Baroque elegance, but in their almost classical form they fit well into the general reticence of the church's style.
In contrast, the choir organ erected under Konstantin von Buttlar is distinguished by exceptionally rich Baroque carvings. Both the altar and the stalls are the work of the Franciscan cabinet maker Georg Blank. In the four corner panels figures of the early Fathers of

the Church, Jerome, Gregory the Great, Ambrose, and Austin, all by Artari.

Next to the southern aisle, to the left of the side portal, is St. Andrew's Chapel. The room was once particularly rich with exquisite stucco ornaments in the most elegant Baroque manner. The cupola, destroyed by a direct bomb hit, was restored in a less ornate style. On the south wall St. Andrew's Altar with a Baroque painting. On the wall before the holy water font a tablet in memory of the tomb of King Konrad I in the church. The location of the grave itself is unknown.

Proceeding along the aisle we notice the ingenious articulation of the space which subdivides the aisles, corresponding to the sequence of the arcades of the nave, into small barrel-shaped passages and chapels crowned by cupolas. In the first oval chapel, with its cupola restored after war damage, symbolic frescoes in the spandrels by Melchior Steidl. Here is the altar dedicated to the Three Magi. It still originates from the old collegiate church and bears the coat of arms of Prince Abbot Placidus von Droste. It is made of precious material with its base of black and red marble, the figures of alabaster and the two upper little columns of agate. The lovely altar piece (1712), the most beautiful in the Cathedral, is by the Fulda painter Johann Ignaz Albin, while the altar itself was built in the workshop of Johann Wolfgang Fröhlicher at Frankfort on the Main. The two delicate alabaster figures represent St. Boniface and St. Sturmius.

The second chapel is dedicated to St. Martin. The altarpiece depicts the two saints by the name of Martin, Martin the Pope and Martin the Bishop. In the spandrels (by Melchior Steidel, like in all side chapels in the Cathedral) allegories of the four cardinal virtues.

In the now following south transept is St. Benedict's Altar designed and executed by Artari. The huge alabaster statue is by Johann Neudecker the Elder. On both sides of the altar allegoric groups of figures representing the triumph of the Church over Unbelief. Above, in the recesses of the corner panels, the figures of the Apostles St. John and St. Andrew, by Artari.

To the right of the altar the sepulchre of Prince Abbot Konstantin von Buttlar (d.1726). Above the galleries in the intersection of the

aisle and the transept medaillons of the Prophets Jeremiah and Micah by Columba.
In front of the central pilaster of the crossing a statue of the Blessed Heart of Jesus from the workshop of the brothers Fleck in Fulda.
Proceeding in the southern aisle left of the High Altar we pass the third, circular chapel with the Holy Cross Altar. The Baroque altarpiece represents a Calvary scene. The stucco decorations are an early work by Andreas Schwarzmann.
We come to the St. Anna Altar at the straight wall at the west end of the south aisle- another work by Artari- with an altarpiece by Christoph Jung. In front of the altar a memorial slab indicating the final resting place of Anna of Prussia, the wife of the Hesse landgrave, who had converted to Roman Catholicism (d.1918).
The staircase on the right leads us down to St. Boniface crypt, the national shrine of the Germans of Roman Catholic faith. Above the staircase a large painting by the Fulda court painter Emanuel Wohlhaubter, representing the martyr's death of St. Boniface.
In front of the eastern wall of the crypt is St. Boniface Altar, richly embellished with alabaster images: the tomb of the Apostle of the Germans.
The altar by Johann Neudecker is the finest work ever created by him. The relief vividly presents the moment when St. Boniface is felled by the murderer's sword, while angels come rushing from the heavens with the martyr's crown and palm-branch even before he has sunk to the ground.
The artist has surpassed himself in the antipendium of the altar table. We are looking, as it were, into the tomb and anticipate the hour of Judgement Day, when the martyr will rise to his eternal bliss. He is of noble and powerful stature. Angels help him to lift the stone lid covering the sarcophagus. But this is only a graceful detail. The heavy stone slab floats away. The last trumpet has sounded. The saintly prince of the Church will gloriously rise from the depth of his grave as a confessor, martyr and apostle of the Church Triumphant. Strong in faith and sure of victory, the message of these images is powerfully impressing.

Mary's Ascension and the Holy Trinity

The crypt is laid out in the form of a cross. The central part is supported by four groups of four columns each. The deep incision by the staircase unfavourably influences the room effect. The recesses in the walls contain sixteen sandstone statues by Andreas Weber (1705–1710). The six figures in the chancel represent holy popes, the remaining ten holy bishops, among them Rabanus Maurus, Fulda's fifth abbot who later became Archbishop of Mainz.

Following an ancient custom the hearts of numerous prince abbots are buried in the walls on both sides of the altar.

We leave the crypt by the northern staircase. Over the exit the statue of the knight Simplicius on horseback from the 14th century. At the straight west wall of the northern aisle is St. Valentine's Altar by Artari. The altarpiece is by the Fulda painter Christoph Jung.

To its right is the entrance to the Lady Chapel, which serves as the sacramental chapel. St. Mary's Altar (erected in 1758) is a graceful piece of work. The two attendant figures represent St. Peter and Magdalene, both in an attitude of repentance. In the four corner panels allegoric figures of the Virtues: Hope, Faith, Love and Strength. Originally executed by Artari, they were re-fashioned in 1774 by the Fulda sculptor Joh. Michael Hois in the Classic taste of the period with rather deplorable results. On the west wall a painting of the Holy Family by Prof. Knackfuß (around 1900). It used to serve as the altar piece for the altar of the saints Crispin and Crispinian that had been re-dedicated to St. Joseph. Opposite paintings by the Fulda painter Klemens Witzel representing the „Annunciation“ and „Mary's Wedding“.

The Lady Chapel used to be the burial ground for the Benedictine monks of lowly birth. From 1802–1854 it was used as a store room, a fact that explains the soberness of the chapel.

From the Lady Chapel we now proceed along the northern aisle, passing the altar to Fulda's patron saints, Simplicius and Faustinus, with a mediocre altar painting , and we come to St. Sturmius Altar in the north transept. This altar, dedicated to the venerable founder of Fulda Abbey corresponds in its general arrangement to the Benedictus Altar opposite. The altar is again by Artari. The allegoric

St. Boniface's death, relief at St. Boniface altar

figures, symbolizing Fulda's Church and the blessings of clerical rule in the Principality of Fulda, as well as the apostle statues in the upper recesses, St. James the Elder and St. Matthew, are by the same artist while the excellent alabaster figure of St. Sturmius was executed by Neudecker. The predella reliefs depict the life of St. Sturmius.

To the left of the altar the sepulchre of Amand von Buseck (d. 1756). Above the galleries bridging the aisle more prophets' images by Columba.

At the north-west central pilaster a bronze statue of St. Peter (the copy of a statue in St. Peter's in Rome). And, diagonally opposite, a recent carving of St. Elizabeth of Thuringia. As well as St. Boniface, she is the patron saint of the Diocese of Fulda.

Proceeding along the north transept we see the altar dedicated to the saints Crispin and Crispinian with an altarpiece depicting St. Crispin's decapitation. The next altar is St. Thomas Altar with a painting by Christoph Jung. Near the northern side portal is St. John's Chapel (also the baptistery), richly decorated with stucco work. Nowhere else in the Cathedral do we find stucco ornaments in such profusion and wealth of ideas as in the two side chapels of the east facade. Unfortunately , the decorations in St. Andrew's Chapel were lost in the war. Standing in the corner niches are the figures of the saints Mary, Joseph, Joaquim and Anna. The images of Mary and Anna are by Artari, the others by an unknown artist. In the chapel Archbishop Dr. Joh. Bapt. Dietz (d. 1959) and Bishop Adolf Bolte (d. 1974) lie buried.

We have come to the end of our round. We have come to know an edifice of imposing beauty and oneness and a Baroque building which in its classical form is unique. We can fully agree with the appreciation by the foremost expert on Fulda's Baroque architecture, Dr. Karl Freckmann, when he writes: „In its classical repose the Cathedral of Fulda has something timeless, something of eternal validity. The Cathedral built over the tomb of St. Boniface was, and still is, a monument of *ecclesia triumphans*“. The forces that made this work a success sprang to a great extent from the Martyr's tomb in

Ragyndrudis Codex, the so-called Boniface crocier and the head reliquy of St. Boniface, Cathedral Museum

IN NO MI NE
DI
SVM MI

its heart, from the history-making life-work of the great saint, and from his blessed importance for the salvation of mankind.

The Cathedral Museum

The museum is accessible both from the Cathedral itself by a portal in the southern aisle next to St. Anna's Altar and by a gate in the wall to the left of the east front bearing the coat of arms of the present bishop, Archbishop Dr. Johannes Dyba, over its lintel. From here you enter Deanery Gardens. A pergola leads you to the museum entrance. Along it fragments of architecture and grave monuments from the old collegiate church covering the periods from the 9th to the 18th centuries. The museum, first opened in 1965, now occupies rooms that have been designed by the architect Michael Brawne in 1994. It contains eminent exhibits: the St. Boniface reliquies (the reliquary with the Saint's head, a manuscript from the saint's possessions pierced by the murderers sword, remnants of his robes), the so-called Boniface Crozier, the great Silver Altar for the embellishment of the High Altar at particularly festive occasions, more excellent works by Augsburg goldsmiths (silver statues, the reliquary with the head of St. Sturmius, antependia, monstrances, chalices and candlesticks), Gothic sculptures, clothwork and sacred vessels, valuable paintings (among others by Lucas Cranach), a unique collection of Baroque clerical vestments of noblest design, colourful appearance and marvellous preservation. No visitor to the Cathedral should miss this magnificent collection.

Annexed to the west side of the Cathedral are the former convent buildings, today the Episcopal Seminary. Opposite these buildings is the former State Library, now the home of the Pontifical Theological Faculty. On the southwestern side of the Cathedral is the Deanery.

ST. MICHAEL'S

History of the Building

St. Michael's was built by Fulda's fourth abbot, Eigil (818–822), and consecrated on January 15th, 822 by Archbishop Heistulf of Mainz. As a burial church it was situated in the monk's cemetery.

Its original structure is of the greatest interest to students of art history: a circular building of 13,5 meters in diameter (15 yards). Its vault is supported by one central pillar in the crypt. In the rotunda above eight pillars arranged in circular form with a passage around them. The dome-shaped vaulted roof ended in a keystone.

Exceptionally many documents about this first building have been preserved by the monk Bruun who wrote a detailed account in his „Life of Eigil" under the pen-name Candidus. The spiritual father of the edifice is Abbot Rabanus Maurus who formulated the titles of its three altars in verses. He interprets the single pillar in the basement and the keystone of the roof as Christ, the eight pillars as the way of the Eight Beatitudes that emanate from Christ and lead the faithful up again to Him. The real architect of the church was the Fulda monk Radulf, successor to Abbot Ratgar, the builder of the collegiate church who had been possessed by his passion for building.

Only the crypt remains of the original building. Probably the rotunda was destroyed in the 10th century and subsequently re-erected, making use of the old pillars and capitals. Significant alterations and considerable extensions happened under Abbot Ruthard (1075–1096). Ruthard added the western nave and short transepts in the north and the south. Thus the rotunda became the crossing of a cruciform church. The rotunda was also extended by adding another storey with a gallery, because the new nave had been given two storeys. This upper storey was also provided with an altar, so that divine services could be held on both floors. Thus the central part now consisted of three storeys altogether. The square Romanesque tower was also erected by Ruthard. Another storey was later added to it which can be dated by its stylistic features to be from the second half of the 12th century. More rebuilding in 1315 gave the nave a steeper roof and a wooden barrel vault to the upper storey. In 1618,

the tower over the rotunda was changed into a steeple. Rotunda and nave were given lancet windows. Around 1716 the interior was given a Baroque appearance by Provost von Clodh and the nave turned into a room with only a single storey. Prof. Lange of Marburg attempted to restore the building and its interior to its original Romanesque shape in 1855. Unfortunately he did too much of a good thing by adding rich portals and a round window to the bell-tower. Some more well-meant attempts at restoration were made until the Fulda senior building official, Mr. Schalkenbach, managed to restore the building essentially to the shape of Ruthard's church of 1092 (1935/36).
St. Michael's is picturesquely located on Michaelsberg which, with its balustered wall, as it were, represents the base for this venerable edifice.

The Outward Aspect

Its outward appearance already conveys rather a clear idea of St. Michael's space articulation. We recognize the cruciform arrangement of nave and transepts and the square apse annexed to the rotunda in the east. Its two rows of windows indicate the two storeys. Among the outward details we notice a Gothic stone lantern in which at certain times an oil lamp burns in commemoration the dead, a small sundial at the gable of the southern transept, the threefold tapering of the bell tower, the use of Carolingian tombstones as corner stones, and the bell arcades typical for Romanesque buildings in the Fulda region. A large slate slab created by Prof. Ewald Matare that serves as a memorial to the dead of World War II has been erected at the south wall of the tower.

The Interior

is best entered by the south portal. In the rotunda our attention is at once arrested by the circle of eight pillars, some of them with valuable, strangely shaped capitals. The cubiform capitals are supposed to be from around 1000 and were made for the load-bearing pillars. The two capitals to the right of the altar (next to the south portal) are Carolingian. Before being used they had to be adapted to the pillar shafts. The true time of origin of the pillars to the right of the

altar (next to St. Rochus Chapel) was difficult to determine. Meanwhile they have been attributed to the same period.
St. Michael's rotunda has essentially been preserved from the times of Eigil (around 820). Alone for the sake of its altar it deserves our whole attention. This ancient building holds its place in German art history as one of the very few Carolingian edifices left to us. Inside the rotunda shaft, in the spandrels above the pillars are remains of Carolingian murals. Another fresco from the 11th century has been preserved above the east apse with the sacramental altar as a rest of those that once covered all the walls of the church. It has been interpreted as the Return of the Lord on Judgement Day with St. Michael escorting the souls. This closely relates to the original use of the church as a cemetery chapel and burial ground.
In the nave Gothic statuettes from around 1500. At the side walls, St. Mary and Catherine (r.), Jerome and Lioba (l.). In the arched passage to the tower, reliefs of James (l.) and Jodocus (r.) corresponding to those in the southern transept (Barbara and Ottilia). All these sculptures are supposed to be wood-carvings from Gothic altars. In the cross-vaulted tower lobby a Baroque statue of Michael the Archangel.
The northern transept is occupied by a chapel erected in 1716 in its present form. In it is a Baroque altar with an impressive Pieta by Andreas Balthasar Weber, sculptor in Fulda since 1704.
The saints Sebastian and Rochus, patron saints who were called on in times of the plague, are found at its side. Of particular interest is an early Gothic stone slab in the left corner of the chapel depicting the Passion of Christ. Some more memorial slabs in the same place are of less interest.
On the wall of the southern transept adjoining the rotunda two Gothic reliefs, Antony the Hermit (l.) and Valentine (r.). On the eastern wall a Gothic Calvary scene (15th century) with Christ on a cross in the form of the Tree of Life.
From the southern transept we descend into the crypt. No doubt it has completely retained its shape from the times of Eigil. The short central pillar with its Ionic capital supports the circular barrel vault.

St. Michael guiding the souls, fresco, 11th century

The altar has been recently erected. The circular passage in the crypt is divided into cells that used to be the charnel house of the monk's cemetery. The crypt contains the stone sarcophagi of Eigil and that of the Iro-Scots monk Amnichad who according to legend lived in the crypt as a recluse.
The upper, not accessible, floor of the church contains remains of Romanesque murals.
No receptive visitor will leave St.Michael's without being deeply impressed by the solemnity of its interior. Still, we ought to remember that it represents no more than a tiny remaining fraction of Fulda's buildings from the Carolingian, Ottonian and Romanesque periods. After all, besides the immense Ratgar basilica, the convent buildings and an imperial palace, the market church and the monasteries on Frauenberg, Petersberg, Johannesberg, and Andreasberg, it was only a cemetery chapel!
Adjoining St. Micheal's is the residence of the Bishop of Fulda.

The eight pillars in the rotunda

THE PALACE

Building History

The first residence of Fulda's prince abbots was a castle begun by Heinrich V von Weilnau and finished in 1312. Already in 1331 it was destroyed again at a rising of Fulda's citizens so that Heinrich V von Hohenberg had to re-build it again. Johann Friedrich von Schwalbach had it pulled down for a new building in the Renaissance style (1607–1612) which from then on was called a palace. The keep, left from the first castle, was given-octagonal shape in its upper part.
The prince abbots Adalbert von Schleiffras (1700–1714), Konstantin von Buttlar (1726–1737) and Adolf von Dalberg (1726–1737), erected the palace as we know it today.
Considerable elements of the old Renaissance building were integrated. The middle block and the buildings in the central court were erected between 1707 and 1717, the left side wing was finished in 1721 after the right one had already been built by 1711. The archi-

tect was Johannes Dientzenhofer; after he had left the town in 1711 Andreas Gallasini finished the palace according to Dientzenhofer's designs. The old tower that had been retained and integrated in the palace was given a platform instead of its helmet under Heinrich von Bibra (1759–1788).
In 1894 the Palace was acquired by the City of Fulda from the Landgrave of Hesse. It now serves as its administrative headquarters.

The Outward Aspect

The Palace imposes not only by its sheer size, but also by its calm, well-balanced proportions. Its facades were renovated in 1979/80 to restore the original colour scheme of the time of its erection.
We enter the outer courtyard by a wide thoroughfare flanked by a wrought-iron, partly gilded fence with rich ornamentation. The six mythological statues of Themis, Mars, Zeus, Hercules, Apollo and Athene are by Johann Neudecker the Elder.
Two flights of stairs at either side wing lead to portals crowned by the coats of arms of Konstantin von Buttlar (l.) and Adolf von Dalberg (r).
The court of honour is concluded by the transverse building accentuated by a sandstone projection and structured by pillars, pilasters, balconies and a thoroughfare. It is crowned by a statue of the goddes Fortuna (a copy of a piece of work by A.B. Weber) whose cornucopia symbolizes the blessings of princely rule. Within the pediment the Schleiffras coat of arms held up by putti.
The buildings in the inner court are accentuated by pilasters with Corinthian capitals and by arcaded lobbies. Opposite the thoroughfare of the central block is a fountain adorned with a statue of Diana together with more mythological figures, designed by Artari and executed by A.B. Weber in 1710. Above the thoroughfare of the transverse building an early Baroque figure of St. Catherine, the patron saint of the former abbots' castle.

The Interior

In the thoroughfare to the inner courtyard are columned arcades. From here we enter the lower vestibule with four sculptures representing the four elements.

A few steps lead down to a hall on the ground floor that used to serve as a summer abode -sala terrena – offering the transition from architecture to nature, from which high french windows , unfortunately often shuttered, lead to the Palace Gardens. In accordance with the paintings executed in the hall it is called the Kaisersaal (the Emperors' Hall): In medaillons beginning with a portrait of Rudolf I in the middle of the end wall, sixteen German emperors from the House of Habsburg are represented. The ceiling frescoes refer to historical events in the life and rule of Emperor Charles VI (1711–1740) who lived at the time when the Palace was built. Four medaillons in the middle of the ceiling glorify Habsburg-Austrian rule. All paintings are by the Fulda court painter Emanuel Wohlhaubter. We are in a room that is most representative of the sumptuous Baroque style. The masterful, exceedingly rich stucco work was executed in the years 1727–1731 by Andreas Schwarzmann. The Herms were made by Joh. Friedr. Humbach, the master of the Flora Vase in the Palace Gardens. In the niches of the hall allegoric sculptures representing Architecture and Horticulture that formerly stood in the gardens themselves (We shall find copies on several more occasions).
Back in the lower vestibule we ascend a staircase to the upper one which has been regrettably spoiled by additions in the time of the Hessian electors. From here, turning to the right, the Palace tower can be climbed in summer time. It has remained of the original abbots' castle, its upper, octagonal part crowned by the typical Fulda balustrade. From its top one can admire the unique panorama of Fulda's Baroque quarters, the Palace Gardens, the city and its surroundings.
To the right of the vestibule is a small hall, the Elector's Room, that today serves as an assembly room. During the rule of Elector Wilhelm II it was re-styled in the Classic taste.
Extensive restaurations- taking a number of years- were carried out in the rooms next to Fürstensaal and in the staircase leading up to it after careful research by the expert Fulda architect Ernst Kramer.
In the course of these restorations a Renaissance window casing as well as a medieval lantern niche from the former abbots' castle were laid bare.
Above the staircase landing is a ceiling fresco of the Goddess of Fame

Kaisersaal (the Emperor's Hall)

by Melchior Steidl. Another fresco by the same artist in the upper vestibule depicts the Fall of Phaeton. The painting was discovered during the recent restorations, but had been severely damaged by the insertion of walls in the room. Fortunately the missing parts could be completed after studying other paintings on the same subject by Steidl.

Along the walls are paintings of Fulda's prince abbots and prince bishops. On the right you enter the large antechamber to the former living quarters of the Hessian heir apparent with the room refashioned in the first half of the 19th century by the Hessian court architect Bromeis.

Our round continues from the vestibule into the Tapestry Room. The tapestries are by Flemish weavers from the 17th century. They represent the Virtues (Courage and Hope) and scenes from the Old

Testament (David playing his Harp, Elias with the Angel, Melchisedech and Abraham). In the room a bricked-up fireplace with Dutch tiles. Above it a portrait of Prince Abbot Konstantin von Buttlar and his coat of arms with a chronogramme (1715).
The next room is the splendid Fürstensaal (Princes' Hall) with its richly stuccoed ceiling by Andreas Schwarzmann. In the large central field a fresco depicting the Olympic gods and in the curvatures ten more frescoes with scenes from Greek mythology, all symbolizing the punishment of human hubris by the gods (all by Melchior Steidl).
The middle of the end wall is occupied by a fireplace with a mirror and the Schleiffras coat of arms above it. The mirror frame and the supraports are modern additions in the Baroque taste.
The walls are covered with Lyons silk tapestry in the same style. The chandeliers from Vienna and the seating are recent adaptations to the Baroque interior.
Along the walls the portraits of Fulda's prince abbots and prince bishops from the 17th and 18th centuries, all by the Fulda court painters Wohlhaubter and Herrlein. The hall is used today as the assembly hall of Fulda's town council, for festive receptions and for chamber concerts.
By the adjoining passage and staircase we descend to the lower floor and the corridor in the south wing. On the right of the passage St. Catherine's Chapel with an animated Baroque altar (altarpiece by J. K. Albin) and ceiling frescoes by Steidl.
The corridor serves as a gallery for alternating exhibitions.

The Chamber of Mirrors and the Walderdorff Suite

Above the entrance to the suit is the Dalberg coat of arms, halberds on the left. In the anteroom the portraits of Fulda court dignitaries and a sedan chair for a lady of noble birth.
We first enter the Dalberg Room, the former dining hall of Prince Abbot Adolf von Dalberg (1726–1737). A large ceiling fresco by Emanuel Wohlhaubter depicts the banquet of the Greek gods in serene elation.
The precious stucco decorations by Andrea Schwarzmann represent buildings erected by Dalberg: the Zella provosty buidings where he had spent a number of years, Fulda's university building, the Church

of the Holy Ghost. The stucco ornamentation in the corners symbolize his princely pastimes: the fine arts, warcraft, architecture, horticulture and hunting, at the same time they represent the seasons. A large portrait of Dalberg by Emanuel Wohlhaubter on the wall opposite the entrance. There are also eight portraits of capitularies, four supraports symbolizing the four continents (copies of paintings by Herrlein), a large Rocaille mirror and an iron round stove with the Buttlar coat of arms. The red silk tapestry as well as that in the following rooms has been made to patterns identical with the originals by the same Lyons weaving mill that had delivered the tapestry in Dalberg's time.
After Dalberg's death his successor had devoted his passion for building and horticulture rather to his summer palace, Fasanery. It was only his successor, Adalbert von Walderdorff (1757–1759), that had the yet unfinished rooms in the south wing finished. Times were not propitious. Several times the Seven Years' War swept across the country. Walderdorff himself had to leave his residence to seek shelter in his town of Salmünster. Finally he took residence in his exclave of Johannisberg in the Rhineland where he also died. He never beheld the beautiful rooms that are now called the Walderdorff Suite.
The adjoining Blue Room served as an antechamber to the following audience room. The ceiling fresco is by Emanuel Wohlhaubter: „The Godess Diana Hunting" in delicate pastel hues. A massive Baroque wardrobe and, opposite, a tall mirror with a Rocaille frame, in front of it a Rococo table with a Chinese vase. A series of narrowly arranged paintings in the taste of the period (many by the court painter Herrlein). The ceiling fresco and the supraports depict hunting scenes and portrayals of cavaliers and hunters. A remarkable painting among them is the „Hare among the Cabbages". There are also two early landscapes with ruins and various animal and flower paintings. Two stuccoed niches are for round stoves.
The following Audience Chamber has a particularly fine parquet flooring and silk tapestry in warm golden and reddish-brown hues. Between the windows a mirror and another Rococo table with a charming Chinese vase; opposite, a fireplace with a richly gilted carved frame. Above it a painting of Volcano with his companions at the blazing smithy. Above the doors supraports by Herrlein (like

in the next rooms): here paintings of elegant ladies and gentlemen in the Classic style, all of them in frames carved by Valentin Schaum. To the right of the door a little portrait of Adalbert von Harstall (1788–1802, d. 1814).

In a glass case on the left Heinrich von Bibra's mitre and a copy of his prince's hat. The ceiling fresco is by Wohlhaubter, it shows an allegory of princely rule, its blessings , its rights and its foundations, the latter symbolized by the four cardinal virtues: courage, moderation, justice and wisdom.

The Green Room is the prince's former bedroom with particularly elegant Rococo stucco ornaments. Above the inner wall is a large Baroque painting, a gift by the Count of Schlitz. A concealed door opens to the valet's room, another to the prince's privet. Opposite the entrance two paintings by Herrlein: „Jacob Struggling with the Angel“ and „Angels Consoling the Prophet Eliah under the Gorse Bush“. A „Madonna with Roses“ by Herrlein's brother Johann Peter and (perhaps a sketch ?) „Christ Expels the Money Changers from the Temple“. Between door and the stove niche copies by Herrlein of Peter Paul Rubens' „Moses strikes Water from the Rock“ and „Moses with the Brazen Serpent“, the latter in reverse. Both originals are in the London National Gallery.

The original of a third copy, „Magdalene Anointing Christ's Feet“ is in the Petersburg Eremitage. Opposite is a painting of St. Joseph. The supraports represent scenes from the Old Testament: „The Archangel Raphael with Tobias being Swallowed by a Fish“, „The Tigris River and the Prophet Eliah Sleeping in the Desert , being Waked by an Angel“.

All rooms have oak doors with richly gilded carvings and the Walderdorff coat of arms with the rampant lion. The Walderdorff suite was furnished within a very short period of time. A great number of craftsmen had joined to equip the rooms with inlaid floors, elaborate carvings for the doors and window casings and with silk tapestries. Plasterers framed the ceiling frescoes and mirrors with delicate ornaments. Gilders adorned the carvings and Roncaille ornaments, Valentin Schaum made the frames. The court painter added his charming paintings. All this was done by order of a prince with an obviously extraordinary taste for the fine arts. All this contributed to a stylistically uniform effect of particularly high rank.

The Cabinet of Mirrors

Its climax is the Cabinet of Mirrors. Such cabinets were regarded the perfect embodiment of princely splendour, particularly as mirrors used to be very costly. The combination of select woodwork, gilt frames for mirrors, and paintings on red silk tapestry has created a room of wonderful harmony. The combination of mirrors and paintings seems to be a peculiarity of the Fulda cabinet.
The room contains 46 small paintings: seascapes, ruins, rural idylls, paintings of horses and battle scenes, mythological landscapes, pictures of forests and hunting scenes, portrayals of rural life, three

oval-shaped landscapes, representations of the four seasons that at the same time represent the times of the day and the four points of the compass, and a supraport with a vedoute of Venice. Ernst Kramer, one of the foremost experts on Fulda's Baroque, has found evidence that most of the paintings were copied from copper etchings. Herrlein's ceiling fresco is an allegory of the coat of arms of the Fulda principality.

The little room beside the cabinet of mirrors contains treasures of a different kind: valuable products of Fulda's porcelain factory. In the glass case on the left different figurines. In the left case, among others, a „Group of Seven Planets", designed by Wenzel Neu for the Hildburghausen factory in Closter Veilsdorf. Neu worked in Fulda from 1764 until his death in 1774. Other objects in the same room are plates, bowls, vases with miniatures in blue hues, and a white tureen, also Chinese and Delft porcelain. The next small room is the Red Galley which serves as a picture gallery. Among others there are flower pieces, still lives by old masters, a beautiful Madonna with Child. Next to the window giving on the street a painting of the Immaculate Conception from the 17th century. Two older paintings in the Dutch manner: a man and a woman , paintings of vases with flowers and doves (perhaps supraports), smaller vases with flowers, the signed portrait of an abbot. Opposite the marble and alabaster fireplace a table with the inlaid Buseck coat of arms and two Chinese vases, above it a mirror. The supraports depict angling scenes in an idealized landscape.

In the adjoining „Study", over the door to the Green Room a large painting: „Jesus is Presented in The Temple" (Herrlein). Eight charming portraits of members of the Fulda court adorn the room. There is also a fan from the Princess of Winterstein's possessions, elegant stucco work in the niche and supraports depicting rural scenes.

In the staircase a Franconian madonna (in the style of the Riemenschneider school) with a remarkable fall of the folds (a loan by a Fulda citizen). Another room follows with three glass cases with Thuringian porcelain.

This again is followed by the Art Cabinet, a room with an exhibition of Fulda porcelain. Over the entrance a portrait of Amand von Buseck, to the left of the door one of the Fulda chancellor Karl Benedikt Welle (J. A. Herrlein). Above the opposite door, the portrait of Heinrich von Bibra (1759–1788) and, to the right, a portrait of a Fulda capitulary. All the exhibited objects are products of the Fulda „Porcellain-Fabrique".

In the short period between 1764, the year of its foundation by Heinrich von Bibra, till its closing down under Adalbert von Harstall in 1789, treasures were created that compete with the products of Meißen, Frankenthal, Höchst and Nymphenburg and that are almost priceless on account of their rarity. Coffee services, with bowls going along with them, show miniature landscapes in delicate grey hues, with pale blue little flowers or in wonderful purple hues. After 1780 the Baroque forms were replaced by severer Classic ones. On the straighter form of cup we find delicate portraits of ancient philosophers in grey hues with purple edgings, also bowls for confectionery; candlesticks in the shape of antique pillars bear silhouets. There are the porcelain medaillons of court dignitaries with their well-executed, recognizable silhouettes. for example of Sigismund von Bibra. There are particularly charming groups of figurines that we consider typical for Rococo porcelain. The „Fulda Musicians" have been created by G. L. Bartholomé, who had been Wenzel Neu's assistant since 1770. Later he had modelled after Frankenthal originals. A set of porcelain with a blue strawberry pattern on white cannelated china bears the stamp of Albert von Harstall and is one of the last series before the closing of the factory „on account of too low economic efficiency". Passing the Dalberg Room again we enter a small room with two more glass cases containing porcelain from Thuringian factories. To the left of the door to the following room a copper etching of Prince Abbot Balthasar von Dermbach (1570–1606).

Our walk ends in the guard room. Its use is indicated by the stucco emblems at the ceiling. The pieces of porcelain exhibited here represent the collection of Dr. Oscar von Waldthausen that the City of Fulda has been able to acquire. This eminent private collection had been kept in Gersfeld before. The collection presents an excellent survey over the products of the Fulda factory in its 25 years of existence and of the styles in which they were executed. It concentrates mainly on articles for everyday use, but it also contains a great number of figurines.

THE PALACE GARDENS

The gardens are effectively laid out with the high terraces in front of the Palace and the Orangery. Originally the park had been shaped in the strict forms of Baroque garden architecture, but in the early twenties of the 19th century under Hessian rule they were transformed into an English-style landscape garden. In the years 1990–1993 the attempt was made to bring the layout closer again to its original Baroque forms, in particular to re-establish the axis between Palace and Orangery terraces with its great fountain. Unfortunately most of the garden sculptures have been irretrievably lost.

The palace terrace is bordered by the kind of balustrades typical of Fulda. Old garden statues stand on either side: Flora in the west and Hercules opposite, both by Neudecker. In front of Kaisersaal two allegories in vivid postures: Architecture and Horticulture (again by Neudecker, court sculptor in Fulda between 1720 and 1722). From the terrace two elegant balustered stairways lead down to the clearly pronounced middle axis with the fountain in the middle of the lower garden parterre.

The garden wall along Paulusallee alternates with a fence and has a wrought-iron gate of excellent artistic quality. In both corners below the Orangery terraces recesses with old fountains and water basins. Back again in the middle axis, a large oval flight of steps leads up to the Orangery terrace. In its middle the Flora Vase, an exceptional work of art by the Bamberg sculptor Daniel Friedr. Humbach (1728). Amid luxuriant flower festoons and playing putti, Flora rises as the personification of all the serene glory that once surrounded her. Triumphantly she holds up a golden lily, the emblem of the then ruling prince abbot, Adolf von Dalberg. Nowhere among all the other sculptures in Fulda has the spirit of the period been caught so perfectly and with such carefree elegance as in this mighty statue that the master has cut from a single block. Quite justifiably, the Flora Vase is regarded as one of the outstanding highlights among Germanys Baroque sculptures.

To the north-east of the gardens there is an idyllic pond peopled with waterfowl, a rose garden with a Baroque basin, and the chestnut avenue leading to Kurfürstenstrasse.

Orangery with the Flora Vase

THE ORANGERY

All secular buildings in Fulda are surpassed in beauty and artistic value by the Orangery building in the northern part of the Palace Gardens.

Building History

The Orangery was erected by the art-loving Konstantin von Buttlar (1714–1726). It was designed by one of the most outstanding architects of the period, Maximilian von Welsch, whose plans were executed (1722–1725) by Joh. Fr. Stengel, the assistant of the prince's court architect Gallasini. As the building was only finished during the rule of Prince Abbot Adolf von Dalberg, his coat of arms in found in the Apollo Hall. The adjoining wing, the Stadtsaal (a concert and assembly hall), was added in 1900.

The Outer Aspect

The Orangery is clearly accentuated by a central building and two side wings, thus corresponding to the three halls within. Its wide, well-proportioned front stands at the north end of the Palace Gardens. It radiates festive elegance with its facade subdivided by pilasters adorned with flower festoons.
The Buttlar coat of arms in the pedestal was made by Mockstatt, the master of the Schleiffras sepulchre in the Cathedral. A. B. Weber executed the vases above the pilasters in front of the mansard roof.
There had been pavillons (1726) on either side of the Orangery that were removed in 1826. Recently (1985 and 1990) they were re-erected in their original form on the still existing foundation walls.

The Interior

The artistic quality of the interior matches its outer aspect, the Apollo Hall in the middle being one of Fulda's most remarkable sights. Schwarzmann executed the stucco work to designs by Pozzi. The ceiling fresco by Wohlhaubter increases the festive room effects. Signed and dated 1730 it represents Apollo in his chariot and the four elements sitting in state among the clouds. The allegoric corner frescoes represent the four continents. The central fresco was painted

Apollo Hall in the Orangery

on an only slightly curved ceiling, but an eleborate perspective makes it seem to have a much greater height.

The other rooms on either side are done in simpler, nevertheless elegant style, again with stucco work by Schwarzmann. Next to Apollo Hall and accessible from there is another charming little room with a ceiling fresco symbolizing the four seasons.

PAULUSTOR
(ST. PAULIS GATE)

Next to the Orangery is the massive Paulustor, erected in 1711 to a design by Johannes Dientzenhofer. It formerly stood between the Palace and the Main Guard House (its original position recognizable by the statues of guardsmen on high pillars between the Palace and the Main Guard House). In 1771, Prince Bishop Heinrich von Bibra had it moved to a position that gives the Baroque quarters their singular unity. At the same time the side tracts were added by Karl Phil. Arnd. It still had only one single thoroughfare until, in the middle of the 19th century, windows in the side rooms were turned into passages for pedestrians and the walls in the thoroughfare removed.

At the townward side the gate bears the statues of Fulda's patron saints, Simplicius and Faustinus and , above the prince's coat of arms, a statue of St. Paul. At the other side is a half-length relief portrait of St. Boniface from the end of the 17th century.

Opposite the gate opening to the Orangery is the bishops' palace, the former seat of the provost of Michaelsberg. This unpretentious, though elegant building has essentially retained the appearance from the time of its restauration by Provost Stephan von Clodh in 1718. Above the portal is the coat of arms of the then ruling prince bishop, Konstantin von Buttlar.

THE FORMER STATE LIBRARY

is at the western end of Michaelsberg. The building now serves as the home of the Pontifical Theological Faculty. It was erected under Heinrich von Bibra on the foundation walls of the ancient monastic school in Late Baroque style between 1771 and 1778 by the architect Karl Philipp Arnd. The elaborate library room now serves as a

St. Paul's Gate

lecture hall. The building, erected at a time when the Baroque spirit had already exhausted its strength, is adorned with a pleasing flight of stairs and an interesting sundial.

THE EPISCOPAL SEMINARY

In comparison, the Episcopal Seminary opposite is the earliest Baroque edifice in Fulda, erected at the time of Prince Abbot Joachim von Gravenegg (1644–1671). The portal bears the date 1668.
This exceedingly large building, the former Benedictine monastery, cannot be completely surveyed from any place. Three large wings adjoining the Cathedral form a pleasing cloistered courtyard. Two more wings west of it were added under Adalbert von Schleiffras. In 1970, at the occasion of extensive restaurations, the facades were

restored in the original colours. The building is rather unpretentious with only three adorning elements, two oriels and the scrollwork portal. The two figures above the portal representing St. Boniface and St. Sturmius are copies from 1890 while the originals have found their place at „Stiftsbrunnen“ in Borgiasplatz. The statue of Christ above the portal's segmental pediment seems to be from the Late Baroque period.
In the Seminary gardens is a modern rotunda devoted to the Holy Trinity. The design is by Prof. Sepp Ruf.

DOMDECHANEI (THE DEANERY)

After walking past the Cathedral front, we arrive at one of the most charming corners in the Baroque quarters, the dreamy Domdechanei-Straße (Deanery Close) with the Deanery . Its two wings form a pretty square and are adjoined by the Deanery Gardens, a little park within balustered walls. The Deanery was built in 1702–1704 by the Dean of the Benedictine convent, Provost Bonifaz von Buseck.
Its architect was the highly esteemed Franciscan master builder, Antonius Peyer, who had also given expert advice on Dientzenhofer's designs for the new cathedral. The fronts are attractively accentuated by Tuscan pilasters and alternating segmental and triangular window lintels and the building stands out by its noble proportions. After having been renovated in the original colour scheme the Deanery has become one of the most precious gems of the Baroque quarters.

Portal of the Episcopal Seminary

DEO OPTIMO MAXIMO
SS: BONIFACIO MART: ET ARCHIEP: ET BENEDICTO ORDINIS FUNDATORI
DIVIS LOCI PATRONIS HANC REGULARIUM HABITATIONEM FUNDITUS EXSTRUI AC FIERI
IMPERY COMES A GRAVENECC ANNO MDCLXVIII

STIFT WALLENSTEIN (THE WALLENSTEIN CHAPTER HOUSE)

Situated between Kastanienallee (a chestnut avenue) and the Main Guard House on Bonifatiusplatz is the chapter house for ladies of noble birth, known as Stift Wallenstein, in a walled garden. This unpretentious palace was erected in 1731 by Baron Ernst Joh. Philipp von Buseck, a brother of the later prince bishop. Later it was occupied from 1802 until his death by the last prince bishop, Adalbert von Harstall, after he had lost his principality in consequence of the secularization of all ecclesiastical states. The Prussian field marshal Blücher was his guest in this house.

Since 1833 the palace has been the home of Protestant noblewomen. For this reason it bears the coat of arms of the founder, Amalie von Görtz, nee Baroness Wallenstein. A secular abbess now heads the institution.

Unfortunately, the appearance of the palace has been spoiled by additions in the 19th century.

ST. BONIFACE MONUMENT

On Bonifatiusplatz we find the monument to St. Boniface, one of the outstanding symbols of Fulda from the 19th century. The vigorous figure of St. Boniface holds up the cross in his right hand and the Gospel in his left. The bronze monument with a height of four meters was cast by the Kassel sculptor Werner Henschel and erected in 1842. The reliefs at its base depict scenes from the Saint's life: his arrival in Frisia, the felling of Donareiche (an oak tree worshipped by the heathen Germans), the foundation of Fulda Monastery, and his martyr's death.

More palaces along Bonifatiusplatz and Schloßstraße form the entrance to Fulda's secular quarters. All of them were built between 1737 and 1739 to designs by Gallasini. They used to be the living quarters of high-ranking court officials. The monumental effect of these buildings is heightened by corner pavillons flanking the en-

The Main Guard House

trance to Friedrichstraße, by their front gardens with balustered walls and Delphinbrunnen („Dolphin Fountain").

Plans had existed to continue the sequence of these buildings into Friedrichstraße, but the only one realized is the Kanzlerpalais (Chancellor's Palace) at the end of that street.

Finally, at the eastern end of Schloßplatz, is Altenstein Palace from about 1770 with its rich Rococo portals and thoroughfare. The interior has Rococo stucco decorations in the staircases and in its rooms. Particularly the banqueting hall on the upper floor has lavish stucco decorations by the Fulda artist Joh. Michael Hois.

NONNENKIRCHE

(The Convent Church of the Benedictine Nuns)

The church and the adjoining convent buildings were erected in the years 1626–1631 by Prince Abbot Johann Bernhard Schenk von Schweinsberg.

The Outer Aspect

The architecture of this church represents the spirit of the Counter-Reformation. The Gothic period had long passed, the time of Renaissance had come to an end, when the building with its single nave was still given high lancet windows with Late Gothic tracery and fan vaults in the chancel. Both gables of the unpretentious rectangular church were erected in the Renaissance style. The portal, built only in 1677, has the scrollwork ornaments of early Baroque and its

Church and convent buildings of St. Mary's Benedictine Abbey

statues represent St. Benedict, St. Scholastica, and Mary, the Mother of God. The situation of the portal in a quiet little lane adds to the restrained character of the building.

The Interior

The hall church has nine bays and its ceiling is spanned by ribbed vaults, each with an ornamental keystone; the exceptionally large keystone in the fifth bay bears the builder's coat of arms framed by massive scrollwork. The chancel is at a higher level than the nave and less wide. The nuns' choir is opposite, at the same level. Between them the nave is reserved for visitors. The chancel has also a ribbed vault. The crucifix suspended above it and the altar front are by M. Lioba Munz, OSB as well as the crucifix on the little side altar on the right. Above the side altar on the left is a realistically executed early Baroque crucifix. At the southern inner wall early Baroque sculptures representing St. Benedict, St. Mary, and St. Scholastica.

STADTPFARRKIRCHE

(the town's main parish church)

Building History

Stadtpfarrkirche rises on ground that has been the site of churches for centuries. We know that a church burnt down in the great fire of 1103. Certainly that building had already existed at the time when Fulda was granted market rights in 1019. Abbot Marquard I (1150–1165) had a Romanesque parish church erected and in the time between 1447 and 1466 a Gothic edifice was built which surpassed today's church in size. Its tower still exists and can be easily identified by its lancet windows. The present church was erected between 1770 and 1781 by the citizens of Fulda under Heinrich von Bibra. It was designed by the Jesuit Johann Anderjoch whose plans were executed by Franz Engelbert Springer.

The Outer Aspect

While the rest of the building is comparatively unadorned it has a richly structured front between its two towers. The north tower still has its Gothic windows. The upper part of the projection bears a statue of the church's patron saint, Blasius, by Valentin Weber. It is the latest of Fulda's Baroque sculptures.

The Interior

The interior is dignified. The aisles are separated from the nave by pillars and the nave itself is structured by five bays with two more bays in the chancel.

The church radiates an atmosphere of quiet, still increased by the dignified serenity of the High Altar. The building was erected at a time when Baroque had passed its zenith: The windows as well as the nave arcades have only slightly rounded arches. The only moderately used stucco decorations have little of the delicate ornamentation of Rococo and almost remind of the scrollwork ornaments of early Baroque. The altars already bear signs of the approaching Classic style. The same is true for the confessionals and the soundboard of the pulpit.

The High Altar with its large crucifix and the two side altars dedicated to the saints St. Boniface and St. Blasius were created by the Fulda court stucco moulder Joh. Michael Hois together with Andreas Wittmann. In the left aisle St. Anthony's Altar with paintings by Joh. Andr. Herrlein; in the predella a portrait of St. Stanislaus Kostka. The altar from 1760 originally was in the Jesuit Church pulled down in 1785. In front of the altar a baptismal font from 1486.

The altarpieces for St. Boniface Altar and the small St. Joseph's Altar at the chancel panel as well as the Lady Altar opposite are later creations by Herrlein. In a recess at the end of the right aisle a larger-than-life statue of St. Antony of Padua.

The ceiling frescoes in the chancel, the nave and the organ loft as well as the paintings of the apostles in the nave are also by Herrlein. They represent David (in the chancel), the Sermon on the Mount, The Expulsion of the Money Changers from the Temple, and St. Cecily. The Classic organ screen is from 1837. The stations of the cross are copies of Herrlein's paintings in the parish church of Großenlüder nearby.

Below the organ loft is the sacramental chapel, elaborately ornamented with arabesques, with turned pillars and putti, and a richly

P

SCHOKO
seibert

decorated Early Baroque altar with the coat of arms of Placidus von Droste. Its altar piece again is by Herrlein. This altar had originally been the high altar of the Benedictine Convent Church. On either side ornate reliquaries; at the wall a silver Madonna with a golden aureole and the globe, on the left a representation of the Five Wounds of Christ. Opposite a very impressive sculpture: a Pieta.

In front of the church is the square „Unterm Heilig Kreuz" („Below the Holy Cross") with a pretty obelisk and with a little fountain (from 1669). At the south end of the square the Kanzlerpalais (the former residence of Fulda's chancellor).
The half-timbered house opposite the church also deserves our attention.

THE OLD TOWN HALL

After its restoration in the years 1968–1970 the Old Town Hall has become a conspicuous feature in Fulda's city. In the course of centuries the house had suffered a lot by many alterations when it came to be used for citizen's homes and business premises and only in our times, after a careful study of old views and hand-written plans, it has been restored to its original appearance from the end of the 16th century.
The Town Hall consists of a half-timbered half with an extraordinary architecture and a red solid building. Its Gothic windows were saved from the old parish church and re-used when the building opposite was pulled down. The arcades are additions from the turn of the 19th and 20th centuries when the ground floor became used for shops. Above the arcade arches are stones bearing some coats of arms with dates from the years of the hall's erection (1530) and later. Between the arcades at the eastern facade is a stone with a red hand symbolizing the right of jurisdiction.
In the little square facing the gable front is a little fountain („Stiftsbrunnen") with the original statues from the portal of the Benedictine convent (1668).

ST. SEVERI'S

The little church on Severiberg is the only remaining building from Gothic times. In 1438 it was built as a church devoted to the Virgin Mary. In 1451 Prince Abbot Reinhard von Weilnau assigned it to the use by the well-respected and wealthy wool weavers guild. As the guild used to celebrate the feast of their patron saint, St. Severus, in their church, it came to be known as St. Severi's.
After the Reformation and the Peasant's Revolt it lay waste for almost a century. The first divine service was held here again in 1615. From 1620 to 1625 it was temporarily used by the Franciscan friars and then by the Benedictine nuns as their first church in Fulda. During the Baroque period it became the Fulda garrison church and its interior was re-fashioned in the Baroque style. These decorations were removed in 1882.
The modest nave has four lancet windows without tracery, the chancel twofold windows with Late Gothic trelliswork and ripped vaults with finely cannelated ridges. The keystone in the middle depicting the Holy Ghost bears the date of 1438.
A remarkable Gothic Madonna, a wood carving from the monastery of Limburg in the Palatinate, is among its interior decorations.

In the street above the church is a fine half-timbered house and, at the corner, the „Haus zum Roten Löwen“ („The Red Lion“) which was first mentioned in documents as early as 1330.

THE MUSEUM BUILDING

(Vonderau Museum)

This large block of buildings was formerly used as the Pontifical Jesuit Seminary. Founded with the money from a generous donation by Pope Gregory XIII it was erected (1584) in the place of the Greyfriars' convent (founded in 1273 and suspended in 1550).The seminary soon experienced a rapid development. Thus more buil-

Statue of the Immaculate Conception, museum building

BEA TA
DEI GENITRIX
VITA DVLCEDO
ET SPES NOSTRA
SALVE

ding was done in 1601 and between 1679 and 1682. In 1732 the court architect Gallasini joined the different buildings together to form the block as we know it today. From 1806 it served as a barracks and a fourth floor was added that meanwhile has been removed again in the course of its recent renovation. In 1884 the City of Fulda acquired the building which was subsequently used for an elementary school. In the years 1986 -1990 the sorely delapidated edifice was totally rebuilt to restore it approximately to the appearance after Gallasini's alterations.
Great pains were taken to make its four hundred years of building history recognizable, e.g. by retaining the military emblem above the portal and the large windows of the classrooms at the eastern side of the courtyard.
In contrast to the usual Baroque preference for symmetrical forms only the North-west corner of the building is elaborately decorated and the main portal is not in the middle of the front. This has its reason in the situation that Gallasini had found: Opposite the Seminary building was the former Greyfriars, later Jesuit church which was only pulled down in 1785. So, only this north-west corner could be fully seen from some open space in front of that church. For this reason only this part was given elaborate decorations with pilasters, balustrades and the heads of putti at the window casings. In the corner panel is a recess with the replica of a statue of the Immaculate Conception. Its base with a chronogramme indicating the year 1729. Also the view of the portal had not been obstructed by the neighbouring church. Above the thoroughfare, in the courtyard, is a good statue of St. Francis Xavier by Christian Josef Winterstein (1732).
Today the former seminary buildings house the collections of the municipal Vonderau Museum. The first floor is devoted to the history of town and convent. The exhibits cover pre- and early history and the 1000 years of ecclesiastical rule as well as the ensuing period of secular rulers. They also deal with the recent past and the home life of the town's citizens in the 19th century. Furthermore it illustrates the development of the town and its industries, Nazi rule and the deportation of Fulda's Jewish citizens and also the town's liberation from Hitler's regime and the unfortunate division of Germany after World War II.

In the east corridor of the second floor the natural history of eastern Hesse is presented in a number of large dioramic showcases while the western part of the same floor exhibits works of art (paintings and sculptures) from Fulda and its vicinity.
A lapidary is in the ground floor of the south wing, exhibiting stone ornaments from buildings, columned wayside shrines and old gravestones.
There is a planetarium in the basement of the east wing.
The two rooms in the north west corner, both consisting of two wings at right angles, are the former seminary refectory and the oratory, They are remarkably lavishly decorated in the Baroque style.
The refectory on the ground floor, today the museum café, has rich stucco work by Andreas Schwarzmann.
Above it, the former oratory. Again, the excellent stucco decorations are by the same artist, the frescoes in the ceiling curvatures of this former private chapel are by Emanuel Wohlhaubter. The numerous paintings represent scenes from the life of St. Francis Xavier, the large one depicting the Saint's missionary activities in India and the one in the centre his assumption to Heaven.
The Classic pulpit-altar between the windows assumes a dominant position. It was once used by the first Protestant community from 1802 in the room of the university building now called Marienoratorium (the Lady's Oratory).
A small altar, originally in the former St. Nicholas Hospital, is at the east wall. The altarpiece by Andreas Herrlein depicts St. Nicholas, above it a hospital nursing scene.

Opposite the museum portal a fountain by Georg Brenninger, a gift by the Karstadt department store.

DIE ALTE UNIVERSITÄT

(The former University Building)

This building, erected by the court architect Gallasini, was originally meant as a replacement of the seminary building that had more or less fallen into disrepair, but it was finally erected and established as

a university. Already at his election Prince Abbot Adolf von Dalberg – a far-sighted and energetic man – had resolved to establish a university in his principality, but had first not been able to carry out his plan. But, after being granted pontifical (1732) and imperial (1733) privileges, the new university was solemnly inaugurated in September, 1744. It began with 272 students, 45 per cent of them from places outside the Principality, and it was organized in the four classical faculties: Divinity, Philosophy, Law, and Medicine.
Called Adolphiana after its founder the university existed until its suspension by the new ruler, Wilhelm Friedrich of Orange-Nassau in 1805.
Already in 1802, by orders of the new ruler, its oratory had been turned over to the newly established Protestant community and it maintained this function until 1902.
From 1805 the building itself served as a college for the training of administration officials. As such it survived several quickly following rules until 1835, when it became the home of a grammar school.

Old University Building: St. Mary's Oratory

Ever since that school left for a new house, it has been used by an elementary school and the municipal adult education centre.

The Outer Aspect

The building consists of three wings that include an open courtyard. The pediment bears the founder's coat of arms held by two lions. The unpretentious portal leading into the former university church is adorned by an excellent statue of the Virgin Mary.

The Interior

The room now called „Marienoratorium" (Our Lady's Oratory) is a hall structured by five window axes. Between the windows pilasters bear a barrel vault with intersecting window vaults. The elaborate stucco work of the ceiling – ribands and acanthus leaves – are by Schwarzmann (1774) and, as well as the frescoes, they go back to the time of erection with the exception of the stucco work and the paintings by Herrlein in the two supraports at the narrow side of the room that are clearly executed in Rococo style (1756). These two paintings represent St. Boniface (l.) and St. Blasius (r.). They do not fit well with the iconographic programme of the room with the life of Mary, the Mother of God, as its general topic. The large ceiling frescoes, all by Wohlhaubter, depict scenes from Mary's life: Jesus conceived from the Holy Ghost, Mary's Immaculate Conception, Mary offered in the Temple, The Annunciation, the Visitation of Mary, and a half-length image of the Virgin above the organ. The frescoes in the window recesses are devoted to the veneration and glorification of Mary and the paintings at the pillars are copies (by different artists) from originals in the parish church at Kämmerzell. Medaillons above them depict saints and rulers that distinguished themselves by their particular veneration of the Virgin Mary.
Another detail worth mentioning is the organ with 16 stops built by Bartholomaeus Brünner from Würzburg, still with its original screen decorated with acanthus leaves.
Today the Lady Oratory is used as a concert and lecture room.

HEILIG-GEIST-KIRCHE

(The Church of the Holy Ghost)

The church was built by Gallasini under Adolf von Dalberg in 1722 together with the adjoining hospital.
Fortunately its front is situated at a little square and it goes well together with the severity of Fulda's older Baroque buildings though it does not lack a certain originality. The interior is decorated in the usual style of the more moderate Baroque churches. It is a hall church with five bays in the nave and two more in the chancel. Its straight east wall is unusual with the vestry behind the high altar not occupying the full height of the wall, so that there is room for lofts on either side of the altar. The altar itself is an excellent work of stucco marble by Johann Clahs of Fulda. The altarpiece depicting the Coming of the Holy Ghost is by Emanuel Wohlhaubter. Two side altars on either side of the chancel, with sculptures of the Virgin Mary and St. Joseph that are later works adapted to the Baroque style.

CHRISTUSKIRCHE

(Christ Church)

Christuskirche was erected between 1894 and 1896 by the architects Hoffmann and Zölftel at the corner of Lindenstraße and Bibraplatz. As a new, independent building it took the place of the former university church that had served the Protestant community so far.
Its ground plan is cruciform with the tower and portal in the west. The unpretentious interior has lancet-shaped arcades and ribbed vaults. The chancel is a little elevated above the nave. The organ is from 1967. At the parapets of the organ loft two cherubs with trumpets and two reliefs depicting David lamenting Jonathan and Christ raising the Youth of Naim from Death.

Christ Church

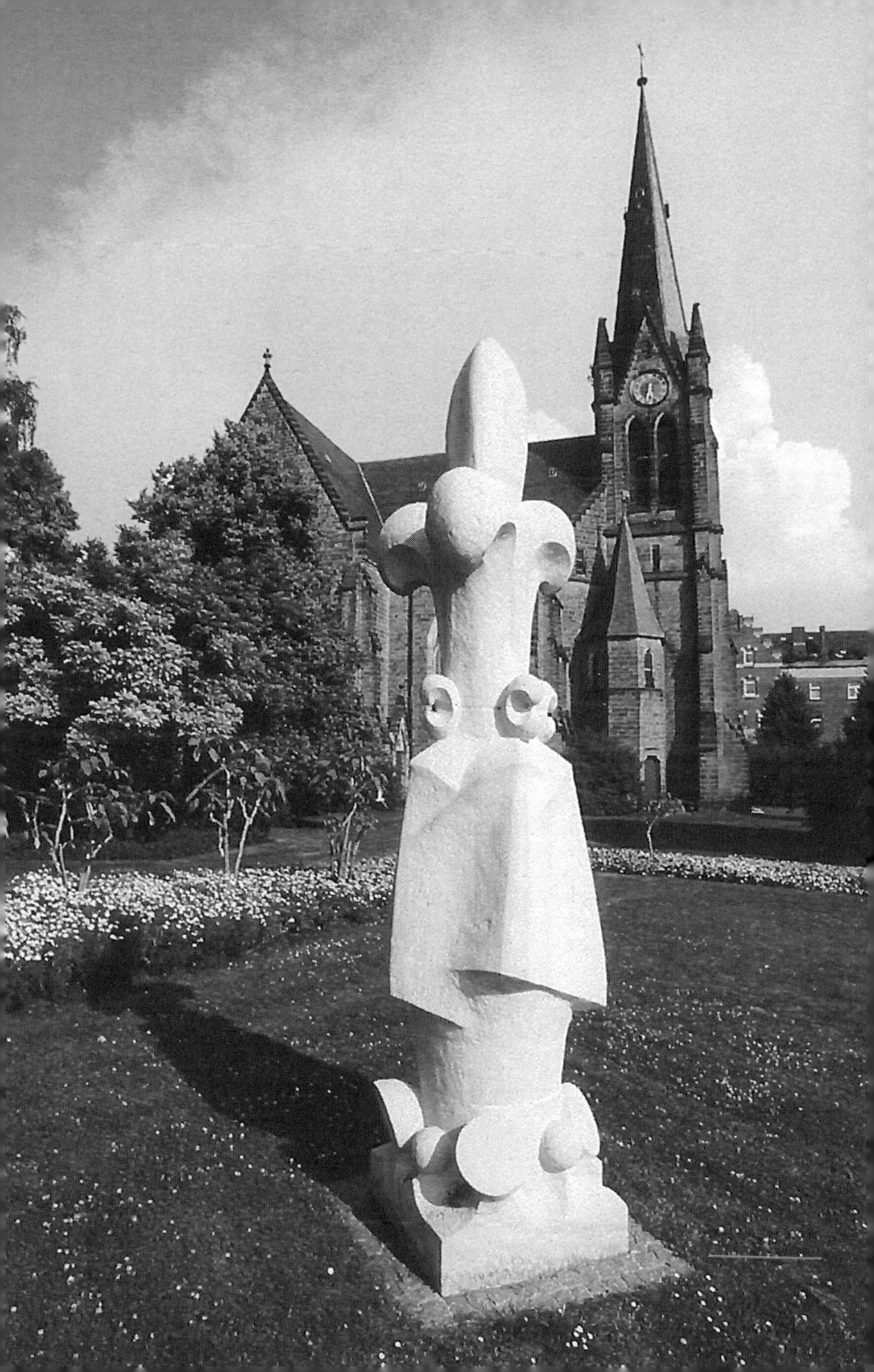

When walking around in Fulda's old quarters one will find a lot more objects waking historical reminiscences and pleasing to the art lover's eyes: remains of the old town walls and their fortified towers, particularly „Heertor“ (one of the oldest town gates in Germany from the 12th century), timber-framed houses, like that next to Hexenturm (the „Witches Tower“), the birthplace of the Nobel Prize winner Ferdinand Braun, a great number of Baroque houses adorned with Madonna statues, also a number of columned wayside shrines. Fulda also prides itself in old and recent fountains, e.g. the old Harstall fountain on Gemüsemarkt or the modern one in Marktstraße.
It would go far beyond the scope of this guide to describe them all in detail.

FRAUENBERG

Among the hills bearing old convents the one nearest to the Baroque quarters is Frauenberg. Within parks and gardens there is the Franciscan convent with its church at the summit. From here the visitor has an unimpeded view of Fulda and the surrounding countryside with the Rhön and Vogelsberg hills in the distance. There are no remarkable works of art but a church built in the spirit of Franciscan simplicity. Nevertheless, its picturesque situation above the town makes it particularly attractive. Nature and architecture together with a number of smaller art objects all contribute to this attractiveness: the hill itself above the Fulda valley and the ancient walls and trees tell tales of old legends and traditions, of works of piety and of the popularity of its Franciscan inhabitants.
Frauenberg hill begins to rise immediately beyond Paulustor. After passing a Baroque columned wayside shrine (1678) at Eichsfeld and an old churchyard a threefold maple avenue leads up the hill. At the upper end of the path is the fine „Pestsäule“.

Frauenberg convent church

Pestsäule

A huge Corinthian column rises from a massive base and bears the image of the Queen of Heaven that Prince Abbot Joachim von Graveneck had erected in 1651. It was to be a monument both commemorating the end of the Thirty Years' War and the great plague in Fulda that had ended 300 years before. Ever since, processions to the

„Hill of Our Lady“ have been held in constant memory of that troubled plague year. The precious statue of the Virgin Mary is one of the few Fulda monuments from the middle of the 17th century. On a crescent moon Mary as the Queen of Heaven holds the Infant Jesus in her right arm, a sceptre in her left and she wears a crown on her head. The symbolic relief sculptures at the base are executed in the scrollwork typical of early Baroque. From here our way leads up the hill to the convent church, between ancient walls and Fulda's only vineyard, accompanied by objects of pious devotion: a crucifix at a tree, a Baroque Madonna in a golden aureole (1730) on the convent wall , weathered ancient stations of the cross and modern representations of the Seven Beatitudes of Mary in small recesses in the wall. Just a little beyond the hilltop a little chapel with a representation of the Souls in Purgatory. Then at last we arrive at the little square in front of the Convent Church and its portal, a spot of almost mediterranean charm.

The Convent Church

was designed by the Franciscan friar Cornelius Schmitt. The simple, nobly shaped facade with its ridge turret is adorned by three sandstone statues: in the lower niches St. Boniface (l.) and St. Rabanus Maurus (r.), in the gable an image of the Immaculate Conception. The walls on either side of the church bear statues of St. Francis (l.) and St. Antony of Padua.

After entering by the massive porch we are surprised by the rich interior. The plain hall church is structured by eight bays, the walls are accentuated by pilasters and large windows. The barrel-vaulted ceiling is accentuated by girder arches resting on volutes and by the intersecting window vaults.

On either side pairs of Rococo statues and altars.

On the High Altar a Madonna much venerated for her miraculous powers arrests the viewer's attention by its position in a canopied niche above the tabernacle. On either side the statues of St. Benedict (r.) and St. Boniface (l.), above, a representation of the Holy Trinity surrounded by angels and putti and over it the coat of arms of the founder, Prince Bishop Heinrich von Bibra. More statues at the further sides represent Michael the Archangel and the Guardian Angel. The wooden

altar itself was carved by the Franciscan friar Hyazinth Wiegand.
In the window recesses on either side of the High Altar side altars dedicated to the Saints Elizabeth and Thekla. On the pilasters next to the altar figures of St. Bonaventura (l.) and Louis of Toulouse.
Then, on the right-hand side of the chancel, St. Francis' Altar with an altarpiece depicting the scene of the granting of the Portiuncula indulgence., the painting above shows the stigmatization of the Saint. The attending figures are those of John of Capistrano (r.) and Bernard of Siena (l.).
Opposite is St. Antony Altar with a painting depicting the Saint interceding for a group of people in distress and above it one of the Infant Jesus. Attending figures represent Petrus Regalado and Peter of Alcantara.
In the recesses facing the High Altar St. Francis and, opposite, St. Antony. The altars in the nave are dedicated to St. Joseph (r.) and Joaquim and Anna. Moreover, there are figures of Franciscan martyrs at both sides of the nave.
The side altars have been excellently done in stucco marble. An expert of this technique, Cornelius Schmitt, had come to Fulda and taught one of the friars to execute the work.

It is remarkable that the Franciscan community had been able also to find a sculptor among their own community for all these rich decorations. The statues were all made by the friar Melchior Egenolf. Another remarkable fact is that all paintings for the side altars and above the confessionals (with the exception of a mediocre one above the middle confessional on the left) were executed by the Fulda court painter Johann Andreas Herrlein. The altarpieces depict the holy nuns Catherine of Bologna with the Infant Jesus, Clara expelling the Saracenes with the help of the Holy Sacrament, Margarete of Crotona experiencing an apparition of the Lord with angels, and Theresa of Avila with her vision of an angel extracting a blazing arrow from her heart. In contrast to the tastes of the Franciscan artists, Herrlein was not devoted to Rococo, but preferred the models of Dutch and Spanish artists, thus introducing a calm and realistic note into Fulda's Late Baroque. In this church the artist proved to be the most outstanding painter of altar pieces in Fulda's Baroque.

The Stations of the Cross

From Frauenberg old stations of the cross lead up to the summit of neighbouring Kalvarienberg („Calvary Hill"). There, in a picturesque spot with stone benches, is a Calvary group as the 12th station. Three stairs lead up to a balustered gallery with angels bearing the tools of Christ's Passion. All figures are in very agitated postures unusual for Fulda's Baroque. The stations of the cross were put up in 1737 by the convent's Guardian, P. Angelus Brinkmann, and executed by the Franciscan sculptor Wenzeslaus Marx from Leitmeritz in Bohemia.
Within the little chapels are paintings of the way of the cross that were renewed and completed at the occasion of renovations. Originally there had also been statuettes that were removed to corresponding little buildings at the outer north wall of the convent church . They can be seen after entering the gate to the left of the portal.

The municipal park on Frauenberg and Kalvarienberg hills gives occasion for leisurely little walks. At the brink of the little pond is a statue of St. Francis by Agnes Mann, erected at the occasion of the 750th return of the Saint's death.

ST. ANDREW'S IN FULDA-NEUENBERG

This former monastery, later provosty church is now the parish church for the district of Neuenberg. Neuenberg is situated to the west of the city, across the Fulda River.

Building History

The building was erected by Abbot Richard in the years 1020–1023 following closely the model of Ratgar's basilica. The ground plan is laid out in the form of a T. Transept, apse and the crypt below have remained almost completely unchanged. Also the lower parts of the nave up to the height of the window sills go back to that time.
A Romanesque three-storied west tower was added. Its bell arcades are characteristic for many Romanesque church towers in the Fulda area. The ground floor of the tower was given a Gothic portal and ent-

rance hall after the church had burned down in 1440, and in 1480 a chapel dedicated to St. John was installed in its first floor that can be reached from inside the church by a spiral staircase. Remains of a Gothic cloister have been preserved at the north side of the church.
A relief image of St. Andrew above the tower portal and the coat of arms of Provost Benedikt von Rindstorff from 1647 at the south side of the nave remind of a restoration at the middle of the 17th century. In 1766 Provost Karl von Fechenbach had the interior decorated in the Baroque style and the tower got its Baroque helmet. In 1954 these decorations were largely removed, but restored again in the years 1984/85.
At this occasion remains of a Romanesque chancel parclose and the tomb of the founder abbot Richard were discovered. A Baroque staircase next to the apse was also found and an arcade arch allowing a view of the crypt opened.

The Interior

We enter the church by the tower portal with its entrance hall. The nave has five bays divided by flat pilasters. The ceiling has a wooden barrel vault interesected by window vaults. It is sparsely decorated with stucco trims around squares in blue and yellow hues.
The transept intersects the nave at full height. From the crossing stairs lead up to the chancel in the apse. There are open arches at the sides of the stairs that allow a view down into the crypt. Immediately in front of the chancel is the re-erected tomb of the founder with a memorial slab bearing the date 1039.
At either side of the chancel stairs leading down to the crypt.
There are only restrained decorations. Under the organ loft are a Vespers image and the remains of murals. Along the walls grave slabs from different centuries. The modest pulpit is decorated with gilt Roncaille carvings and bears the coat of arms of Provost von Fechenbach. Also on the right-hand wall an image of the Virgin Mary with the Pierced Heart. Above the triumphal arch again the Fechenbach coat of arms and above the apse the Eye of God.
The predella of the high altar has decorations with Renaissance and Early Baroque elements. It bears the date 1647 and is a gift from Provost Matthias Benedikt von Rindtorff (1640–67) whose coat of

Frescoes in the crypt of St. Andrew's

arms it bears. The altarpiece shows the martyr's death of the Apostle Andrew, painted by the Fulda court painter Hans Klemp, to the left and right the Roman martyr brothers John and Paul represented as knights. The smaller paintings at its sides portray two more Roman martyrs, Protus and Hyazinth. The tabernacle is a modern enamel work by the Benedictine nun, M. Lioba Munz, from the Fulda convent.

A large painting hangs at the northern end of the transept wall, „The Annunciation". Below it the tomb of Provost Bonifaz von Buseck (d. 1707) and more grave monuments for the provosts Schott von Memmelsdorf (d. 1592) and von Hochstetten (d. 1683). At the opposite end wall a badly preserved painting of a half-figure with a sword and a palm leaf emanating from its mouth. A crucifix by Herrlein hangs at the south wall of the transept. Below it the monuments of the provosts von Rosenbusch (d. 1724) and Specht von Bubenheim (d. 1755).

From the stairs leading down to the crypt an open arch allows a view of the remains of the chancel parclose. Here fragments of paintings in the al-secco technique have been preserved. One can recognize seams of robes, the feet of standing or sitting persons and painted curtains.

The crypt is particularly worth seeing on account of its extraordinarily well preserved murals. It is a square room with four pillars with Attic bases and cubiform capitals and it has three narrow windows. The murals are excellently adapted to the shape of the vaults and the other architectural elements. The state of preservation and the freshness of the colours that were painted at about 1023–25 are satisfactory, even if parts, particularly around the windows, have been lost. The noble serenity, the monumental lay-out, and the execution of the paintings are really impressive.

At the apex of each window Christ was, or still is, depicted; to the right and left in medaillons and in the middle in a mandorla. At either side are, or were, representations of forerunners to the Sacrifice of the Mass from the Old Testament: Cain and Abel with Abel' sacrifice (l.) and Melchisedech's sacrifice (r.).

There are medaillons of Christ and some saints at the ceiling. At the walls and in the spandrels 22 figures of angels holding staffs, balls and discs of unknown symbolism.

Adjoining the north side of the church are the east and north wings of the former convent buildings, now used as a parish centre, while of the west wing only the foundation stones have remained. The three wings together with the church walls had once formed a cloister and the inner yard.

A few steps away from St. Andrew's is Bonifatiushaus (a house for spiritual exercises and church conferences) with its chapel. At the outside wall a bronze sculpture of St. Boniface by H. Söller, Schweinfurt.

THE GERMAN FIRE BRIGADE MUSEUM

The museum was erected in Fulda-Neuenberg in 1976. It is the largest of its kind in Germany and shows the development of fire fighting and fire prevention from the 16th century to our times. The exhibits comprise fire engines from the 16th to the 19th centuries (Hall 1) and the 20th century (Hall 2) as well as smaller fire fighting equipment, uniforms etc. There are also special collections dealing with different aspects of fire fighting.

JOHANNESBERG

The Church

Building History

A church dedicated to St. John the Baptist and St. John the Evangelist was consecrated in 811 by Archbishop Richulf of Mainz. It had been erected by Abbot Ratgar of Fulda and was added to by Rabanus Maurus (822–842) who also founded a monastery and transferred the reliquies of the saints Venantius, Urbanus and Quirinus to Johannesberg where these reliquies remained until the Peasant's Revolt in 1525, when they disappeared without trace. Archeological evidence proves that the church from the 11th century had been a basilica with three naves. There are even traces of two Carolingian predecessors that were found in 1977. Compared with the present church, the one from the 11th was larger. Its tower has remained, though its upper parts were altered in the 12th and 13th centuries. After a fire in the last third of the 12th century the church was newly consecrated. From that time a recently (1990) discovered Romanesque portal at the southern outer wall has remained. Obviously it had served as the access to some adjoining building.
At about 1500 the old church had to give way to a new building for which the existing walls were used, though. This Late Gothic church was redecorated in the Baroque style between the years 1686–91:

the vault was altered, the windows were given a different shape after removing the tracery, and new altars were installed.
More alterations happend under Provost Konrad von Mengersen (1715–1753). Quirinus Chapel was added and consecrated in 1741 and in 1744 an additional eastern facade was built and the tower got its helmet.

The Interior

We enter the church by the Romanesque portal in the tower from the 11th century. The ground floor of the tower with its ribbed vault serves as a vestibule. A second Gothic portal is the entrance to the nave.
The church consists of one single nave with five bays and the chancel with a five-sided apse separated from the nave by the chancel arch. The wooden ribbed vault rests on Early Baroque festooned corbels. The chancel arch bears painted decorations and an inscription reminding of the alterations and the new altars installed by Provost Bernhard von Buseck (1656–1700). All present altars are from that time. The one to the right of the chancel arch has an altarpiece depicting the Annunciation, above it a Madonna statue. The painting for the altar to the left shows the Descent from the Cross with a stucco ecce- homo sculpture above. There are Classic reliquaries on both altars.
The pulpit with its turned pillars and its putti is from the same period (1686). Under the pulpit a beautifully carved door from the same time. The particularly effective predella of the high altar includes the entrances to the vestry behind. The entemblature is supported by turned pillars with Corinthian capitals. The excellent Early Baroque altarpiece depicts the decapitation of St. John the Baptist and above it is a painting of Jesus' baptism in the River Jordan. Over it the coat of arms of the last provost Ludwig von Schönau (1795–1802), who had the flanking Classic vases added. The tabernacle is also a later addition. Above the vestry entrances statues of St. Boniface (l.) and St. Blasius (r.). The high altar and both side altars are by Johann Valentin Neudecker.

Johannesberg, the interior

To the left of the chancel a remarkable monument to Provost Friedrich von Buttlar (1702–1715) and to two more members of the Buttlar family by the sculptor Mockstatt, that were erected by orders of Prince Abbot Konstantin von Buttlar (1714–1726).
To the right of the chancel arch a wooden model for an epitaph to Provost Konrad von Mengersen whose passion for building had changed the appearance of all provosty buildings by refashioning them in the Baroque taste.
The base of the new altar rests on pillars from the 11th century that were discovered during the excavations in 1977. Two more finds from these excavations have been used for the sideboard at the left back wall of he chancel arch. Its top consists of an altar base (turned upside down), under it the foundation stone of the preceding building with a cross and the letters D and B. The organ parapet is divided by volutes and festoons into squares with paintings of the Lord and the Twelve Apostles.
Quirinus Chapel at the south side of the nave was added under Konrad von Mengersen and consecrated in 1741. The large altarpiece shows the martyr's death of Quirinus, the Bishop of Sissek (d. 308). In the spandrels frescoes of the saints Rabanus Maurus, Pope Zachary, and Boniface. In the rounded panel niches unusual half-length sculptures of the four Evangelists. There is also a finely made Baroque confessional and in the middle of the room a Baroque baptismal font with the Buttlar coat of arms.

The Provosty Buildings

The buildings next to the church had been in a deplorable condition for tens of years and the formerly harmonious garden layout with terraces, flights of stairs, balusters and sculptures could hardly be recognized any more. Everything seemed to be doomed to ruin. Then, in 1980, an organization was founded, the „Deutsches Zentrum für Handwerk und Denkmalpflege“ (the German Centre for Crafts and the Preservation of Historic Monuments). Its purpose was to establish a training centre for craftsmen occupied with the preservation of historic monuments. Here bricklayers, plasterers, carpenters, cabinetmakers, painters, tilers and members of similar crafts learn

long-forgotten technologies. The organization occupies the palace and its annexes.
Elements from the old buildings can still be found: bricked-up cloister windows with round arches and fragments of Gothic tracery, Renaissance window casings and a Gothic spiral staircase within one of the buildings. Extensive Baroque alterations of the premises were made by Provost Konrad von Mengersen in 1726 and later. The Roter Bau (The Red Palace) bears his coat of arms above the portal with a chronogramme indicating the year 1727. The red sandstone building was erected by Gallasini in the years 1726–1733. The house with its well-balanced architecture has the provosts living quarters with stucco work and ceiling frescos in some rooms on the first floor and a banqueting hall on the second richly decorated in the same taste.

FASANERY PALACE

(formerly called Adolphseck)

This former summer residence of Fulda's prince bishops can be reached either by Frankfurter Straße or Berliner Straße, and the Fulda district of Bronzell. From Bronzell a long avenue leads directly to the palace.
Though the building contains elements from an older edifice (the second transverse block in the inner courtyard from the time of Prince Abbot Adolf von Dalberg, 1726–1737) it nevertheless must be solely regarded the creation of Prince Bishop Amand von Buseck (1737–1756) and his court architect Gallasini. Buseck did not distinguish himself as a builder in the city itself, but he was no less possessed by a passion for building than his predecessors. It is to him that we owe some of the most eminent Baroque edifices in the Fulda area outside the town itself. They are those sensitively laid out grounds that excel by their harmony of architecture and nature.
The avenue leading up to the palace already arouses expectations of what is to follow. Between gate houses and pavillons we enter the park. Between two guard houses the road leads on into the outer

courtyard with cavaliers' quarters on either side. Then we approach the court of honour through a thoroughfare in a curved balustered wall flanked by four pillars topped by vases. The side wings have corner pavillons flanking the yard and more pavillons next to the adjoining transverse wing with large hall windows in the middle and a thoroughfare below. The tastefully shaped gambrel roofs add to the general effect of this building complex.

A park of 40 hectares is open to the public. Nothing has remained of the Baroque layout. A few features, the pond in front of the south wing and its Classic front, the Baroque flight of stairs and tea pavillons in the Classic taste convey an idea of what once had been. But also today's landscape garden with its clusters of immense trees, dreamy ponds and moss-covered stone benches is full of charm. It is at its best in spring with cowslips blooming and in autumn with the incredible blazes of colour from the leaves of manifold kinds of trees.

The Interior

After considerable war damages the interior has been turned into a museum by its owner, the Landgrave of Hesse. Its visit must be strongly recommended. The rooms and halls with their stucco work and their ceiling frescoes – particularly the Kaisertreppe (the Emperor's Staircase)- as well as the rooms as such that have been altered by the Elector Wilhelm II's court architect, Bromeis, are worth seeing.

The rooms have been richly furnished according to their functions as state rooms or living quarters with furniture, paintings, tapestries, sculptures and carpets.

The palace also contains a considerable collection of Greek antiques and another collection of German and European porcelain that can be seen in a separate guided tour.

PETERSBERG

Among all the sights in Fulda's close vicinity the ancient church on Petersberg hill deserves the first rank. From its hilltop a wide panorama of both the Rhön and Vogelsberg Mountains offers itself to the view as well as the wide Fulda valley and the mighty hill of Rauschenberg nearby.

History

Petersberg looks back at a distinguished, venerable history. It was Fulda's fifth abbot, Rabanus Maurus (822–842) who founded a monastery and a church on the hill. In 835 the mortal remains of St. Lioba were solemnly translated from the Fulda abbey church to Petersberg. In the years 842–847 Raban himself lived in its convent, devoting all his time to studies and monastic life. This was the time between his resignation from the office of abbot and his elevation to the archiepiscopal seat at Mainz.
Shortly after 915 the place was devastated by the Huns, so that the church had to be rebuilt by Abbot Haicho (917–923). Later centuries saw more devastation and rebuilding, e.g. after the rising of Fulda's citizens in 1331 and the Peasants' Revolt in 1525, and even several times during the Thirty Years' War (1618–1648). In 1802 the provosty was secularized and in our times nothing of the ancient convent buildings remains.

Building History

Petersberg's church has a history of over 1000 years. Even a fleeting look at its exterior shows Romanesque, Gothic, and Baroque traces. According to an old tradition (not proved with certainty) the crypt already stood at the time of Fulda's abbot Baugulf (779–802). Three barrel-vaulted niches have been preserved from this oldest edifice in the basement of today's church. The third of these niches had a semicircular apse of which the foundations were discovered in the course of excavations. Under Rabanus Maurus (822–842) a three-naved basilica was built of which the basement of the west tower, the crossing with its arches and the northern side chapel (l.) have remained.

St. Peter's, the interior

The original portal arch as the main entrance to this Carolingian edifice can still be recognized from the outside and, within, the tower chapel archivault and import of the same portal still exist.
After the serious damages by the Huns an extensive restauration became necessary under Abbot Haicho (917–923). At that occasion the chancel apse and the central niche in the crypt were replaced by a straight east wall. The place of the Benedictine monks was taken by a collegiate chapter of secular canons.
In Romanesque times Provost Reginfried enlarged the southern chancel chapel and added a fourth niche to the crypt. A little later Provost Gundelaus had the upper part of the chancel square rebuilt in octagonal shape and a tower was built over the original entrance hall. In spite of these changes it is likely that the three naves from the time of Raban have remained unchanged.
Nothing influenced the appearance of the church more than the changes in the Late Gothic period, mostly by Provost Winkin von

Küchenmeister. The original interior with its three naves was turned into a Gothic hall and the walls of the aisles were made higher as the steep saddle roof that had covered the building so far did not agree with the new proportions any more.
The Baroque period has not essentially changed the aspect of the building. Instead of its high steeple, the octagon above the crossing was given a helmet. Provost Otto von Riedheim had the portal refashioned in the Baroque taste (1685) and Leopold Specht von Bubenheim erected the walls now surrounding the church, thus favourably improving the total aspect of the church. After the Secularization in the 19th century the surrounding convent buildings were pulled down.
Extensive restaurations were carried out in our century, the last one in 1971–75.

The Interior

is entered by the steep stairs that lead up to the nave. In the tower chapel a baptismal font from 1510 and a modern Way of the Cross by Prof. Sauter, Kassel.
We have now entered a hall that gets its light from high Gothic windows . The east wall that separates the nave from the transept and the crossing still remind of the Carolingian three-nave columned basilica. The triumphal arch with its imports has been preserved from Raban's time. The wooden coffered ceiling is covered with manneristic flower paintings and ornaments from the early 17th century. There are five oval paintings from that period: in the centre an Annunciation; the four smaller ovals have portraits of four Fathers of the Church that had particularly promoted the veneration of the Virgin Mary (St. Anselm of Canterbury, Ildephons of Toledo, Isidor of Sevilla and Gregory the Great).
At the side walls Baroque predellae. The south wall bears a huge image of St. Christopher , probably from 1479.
Two Romanesque reliefs at either side of the triumphal arch are most remarkable: to the right, Christ the Saviour enthroned on a rainbow, to the left, Mary the Queen of Heaven with the Infant Jesus and a lily. There are more reliefs from the same period at the south wall of the nave, one of St. Boniface and a fragment of one showing St. Pe-

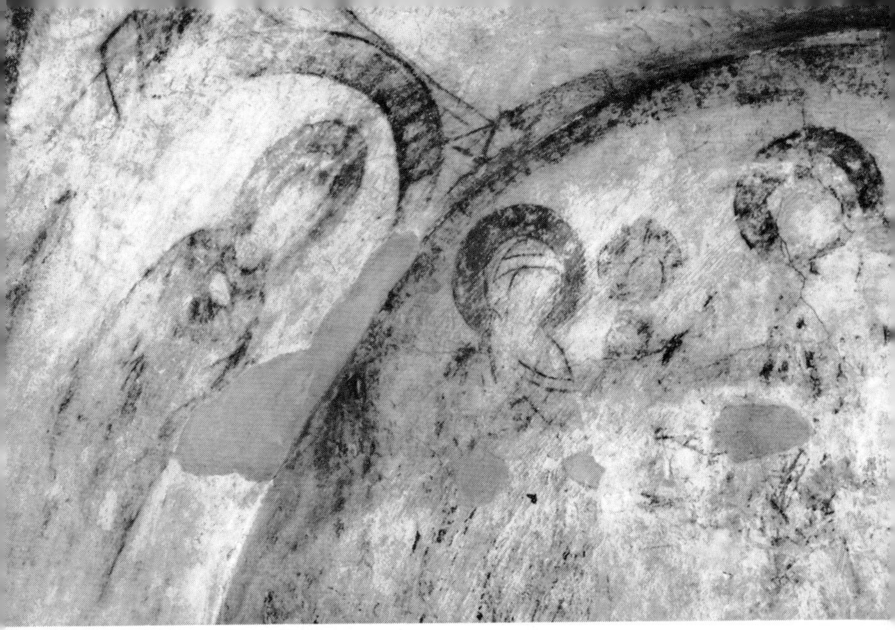

Petersberg: crypt frescoes: Jesus offered in the temple

ter receiving the Keys of Heaven. Furthermore there are reliefs below the pulpit of Karlmann (?) and Pippin (?) and one depicting a stag chased by hounds as the symbol of the soul endangered by sin. The similarity of these reliefs from the 12th century with medieval illuminations is striking. They are among the rare monuments of early Romanesque sculpturing and are of the highest value to art history on account of their majestical, solemn beauty and their excellent state of preservation.

In front of the crossing an ambo, its front a Romanesque blind window framed by chequered ornaments again surrounded by an ornament of twisted ropes. At the back the stone bears the coat of arms of Provost Wilkin von Küchenmeister with the date 1479. The square crossing in the chancel rises into octagonal shape further up. The arcade arches with their elaborate Romanesque columns and capitals were only discovered in 1928.

The chancel itself, once a semicircular apse, is now a square room with a barrel vault. The high altar (from about 1700) has a later altar piece from about 1900.

Wasserkuppe, the highest Rhön mountain

In the southern side chapel a splendidly carved Baroque altar, perhaps the best remaining instance of Fulda's wood carvings from that period.

There is also a great number of grave monuments along the walls of the nave and the crypt.

The crypt is entered by stairs on either side of the nave or by a door at ground level in the south wing of the transept. It consists of three barrel-vaulted niches and a corridor. The middle niche was the place of the tomb of St. Lioba from 833 to the end of the 15th century. A fourth niche was added south of the others by Provost Reginfried and dedicated to the Apostle St. John. At the back wall is

the stone sarcophagus of St. Lioba with a bronze lid (by M. Lioba Munz, OSB, Fulda). Above it a glass case with the remains of the wooden coffin in which St. Lioba was translated to Petersberg from Fulda. At its side reliquies of the saints Boniface, Sturmius, and Lioba. In 1995 the shrine with the head of Lioba, that had been in the custody of Fulda Cathedral for centuries, was solemnly returned to the crypt. The shrine is another work by M. Lioba Munz.
The altar front in the central niche is formed by the one already used by Rabanus Maurus. Its inscription says that it once had been dedicated to the Holy Virgin and Mother of God and to all holy virgins. In the left niche an old altar table from the former high altar in the

nave. Originally a long-lost altar in the niche had been dedicated to St. John the Baptist and to the Prophets and Fathers of the Old Testament. The altar front in the right niche has been turned into a Romanesque window casing in the basement of the southern nave. Parts of its inscriptions can still be read. The altar title refers to St. Michael the Archangel and all Angelic Hosts. The murals in the crypt are unique in art history. They can only be seen well enough in artificial light. There is proof that the paintings in the niches are the oldest on German soil.

The titles of the original altars in the apse and the re-found altar tables agree completely with still existing poems by Rabanus Maurus who describes the murals in exact detail. These murals are supposed to be from 836, or 846 at the latest. In the middle niche St. Mary with the Child in a mandorla, in the vault female (l.) and male (r.) saints, on the girders medaillons with more saints. In the apex of the left niche Jesus' Baptism in the River Jordan with, probably, St. John the Baptist on his left and an angel holding a gown on the other side. Above the altar the Lamb of God and at the sides the figures of prophets. In the corridor vault between the middle and the left niche probably the Annunciation to the Shepherds in the Fields of Bethlehem, and the painting on the wall opposite the left niche seems to depict Jesus' Offering in the Temple. On the left side wall of the right niche (the original vault and the right wall do not exist any more) the figures of angels.

There is proof positive that the decorations in the crypt, both the murals and the altar front, doubtlessly have already existed at the times of Rabanus Maurus and St. Lioba.

EXCURSIONS INTO FULDA'S VICINITY

It goes beyond the scope of a city guide to give a detailed account of the many sights in Fulda's vicinity. Only a few places of interest within a comfortable driving distance from the town can be mentioned here.

Nature lovers and hikers will enjoy the unique countryside and the scenic beauties of both the Rhön mountains to the east and south

and the Vogelsberg hills to the west of Fulda.
Coffin-shaped Milseburg, the most remarkable mountain in the hilly parts of the Rhön with its Calvary group on its top offers a wide view of the green surrounding countryside. Wide open spaces on the high plateaus will prove ideal for hiking. Wasserkuppe, the highest mountain in Hesse (950 m), is the cradle of motorless flying that began here in the early twenties. A museum that exhibits numerous gliders from the earliest types to the most advanced is well worth a visit. Gliding can be watched every day.
Kreuzberg in the Bavarian part of the Rhön is Franconia's „Holy Mountain“ with its pilgrimage church and a litle Franciscan convent that still brews its famous beer.
Extensive moors (The „Red“ and the „Black Moor“) on the high plateaus with their unusual flora – remains of the ice age- offer rewarding observations.
Little market towns, like Gersfeld, Hilders and Tann in the Hessian parts, Geisa in Thuringia and Fladungen and Bischofsheim in Bavaria, are also worth seeing. Gersfeld is a climatic health resort offering Kneipp cures. Tann prides itself in its ancient town gate and three old castles and, particularly, its museum village. Here houses and barns typical of the area have been re-erected and peasant life in past centuries can be studied by its many exhibits within the buildings. Fladungen has a similar museum. A number of villages like Poppenhausen, Wüstensachsen and Hofbieber attract holiday makers.
Those who prefer the comforts of health resorts should visit Bad Salzschlirf (to the west of Fulda) with its brine indoor swimming pool and an attractive little spa garden and Bad Brückenau in the Bavarian Rhön. It was founded by Fulda's prince bishops Amand von Buseck and Heinrich von Bibra and was much preferred by the Bavarian King Ludwig I in the 19th century. Baroque and Classic buildings within well-kept gardens remind of these periods.
Visitors interested in sports will appreciate the two golf courses at Hofbieber and Praforst near Hünfeld. There are a great number of swimming pools and tennis courts in many of the larger places.
Those who prefer winter sports find pistes for both downward and cross country skiing with ski lifts in many places.

INFORMATION FOR VISITORS

Tourist information	Städtisches Verkehrsbüro, Schloßstraße 1 Tel. 1045, 1046, 1051
German Rail	Information Tel. 18–1
First aid	emergency number 112
Police	emergency number 110
Ambulance	Tel. 73303
Lost property	Unterm Hl. Kreuz 1, Tel. 102–0
Divine services	Catholic: Cathedral, Sun. 7, 8, 9.30, 11.30 and 18.30 Protestant: Christ Church, Sun. 8 and 10
Hospitals	Städtische Kliniken, Pacelliallee, Tel. 84–1 Herz-Jesu-Krankenhaus, Buttlarstr. 74 and 76, Tel. 15–1 Clinic Dr. Poeschel, Tel. 55076
Museums	Vonderau Museum, Jesuitenplatz 2 daily 10–18 h, closed on Monday Historical Rooms in the Palace Mo – Thurs. 10–18 h, Fri 14–18 h. German Fire Brigade Museum 10–17 h, closed on Mo. Cathedral Museum, Tues. – Sat. 10–17 h, Sun. 12.30 -17.30 h (Apr. 1st – Oct. 31st), Tues. – Sat. 10 -12.30 and 13.30–16 h Sun. 12.30 -16 h in winter; closed on Monday Hesse State Library, Showrooms Mon. – Fri- 10–12 h and Mon. – Thursday 14 -16 h Fasanerie Museum, Apr. – Oct. 10–17 h, guided tours every half hour

Swimming pools	open air:	Sportbad Rosenau, Jahnstraße Schwimmbad Petersberg, Pfaffenpfad
	indoors:	Zentralbad, Heinrich-von Bibra-Platz Sportbad Ziehers, Magdeburger Straße Rhöntherme Künzell, Harbacher Weg